Introducing

the

EXISTENTIALISTS

Introducing

the

EXISTENTIALISTS

Imaginary Interviews with
Sartre, Heidegger and Camus

ROBERT C. SOLOMON

HACKETT PUBLISHING COMPANY
Indianapolis • Cambridge

Printed in the United States of America
First printing

For further information, please address
Hackett Publishing Company, Inc.
Box 55573, Indianapolis, Indiana   46205

Library of Congress Cataloging in Publication Data

Solomon, Robert C
  Introducing the existentialists.

  Bibliography: p.
  1. Existentialism. 2. Sartre, Jean Paul,
1905-   3. Heidegger, Martin, 1889-1976.
4. Camus, Albert, 1913-1960. I. Title.
B819.S578   142'.78   80-26838
ISBN 0-915144-47-6
ISBN 0-915144-38-7 (pbk.)

for Andy

for Jon, Julie, and Jem

for Kris

and in memory,
Jean-Paul Sartre
(1905–1980)

CONTENTS

PREFACE

"And if he were here, what would he say now?"

—Jean-Paul Sartre
(after hearing that his longtime friend Albert Camus had been killed in a car crash, January 4, 1960)

A few years ago, I was discussing (which is to say pleading on behalf of) a book I had written, with an editor of *The Village Voice.* "But it's sort of existentialism," she half-asked, half-asserted. I said yes. "I thought that went out of fashion years ago," she mused, ending the conversation. (Soon after, she became an editor at *Vogue.*) But the point stuck in my mind—to some people philosophies are merely the intellectual hemlines and pop songs of the season.

It is true that existentialism, as it first came into fashion in Europe, was the product of a very special set of circumstances: the German occupation of Paris in 1940, the growth of the French Resistance, and the moral chaos that inevitably followed the end of the war. In the United States, existentialism was imported by so-called "beatniks" in the 1950s along with espresso coffee, beads, marijuana, and the word "absurd"; exploited by Norman Mailer to justify a character (himself) whom he called "the Hipster"; and tossed about in colleges and some high schools as an antidote to the dullness and conformity of the Eisenhower years. But existentialism has always been more than the fashions it has inspired. Whereas it may promote a set of ideas that are particularly attractive to young people during a period of turmoil (although all periods now seem to be periods of turmoil), and it may well encourage a manner of thinking that places an inordinate amount of concern on "finding oneself" and on challenging if not rejecting God, country, family and all established values, the philosophy is not, as it is sometimes said to be, an adolescent's ideology, and it is certainly not just a thing of the past.

Whatever its European origins, existentialism has always seemed to me to be a philosophy particularly suited to the American sensibility, in its emphasis on immediacy and on action (or at least, *talk* about action or *talk* about talk about action), in its extreme individualism, and in its fanatic concern for true self-identity, self-improvement and, not least, self-righteousness. I have been teaching this philosophy in colleges and universities for more than fifteen years, and it is obvious that Camus and Sartre, for example, continue to excite crowds of students as they did in the 1950s, when their philosophy was something new and fashionable. And since his death a few years ago, Martin Heidegger has also begun to attract a remarkable number of devotees despite the great difficulty of his work. Accordingly, these figures should no longer be considered exotic imports whose ideas are to be studied as a philosophy that is foreign to us. Rather, they have become sufficiently established to be treated as compatriots, to be taken seriously as *our* philosophers. Like Descartes and David Hume, they have now been absorbed into the American philosophy curriculum.

In the following mock interviews, it will be quite evident that I have considerably Americanized these great philosophers. In introducing their sometimes difficult philosophical jargon, they have been made to speak our language. In addition, I have tried to make them accessible and human—men with exciting ideas rather than, as in many recent treatments, oracles without faces, bodies, mannerisms, or humor. There is, of course, no way to present the total picture in a few pages, and I do not pretend to be thoroughly "objective" —which is one of the advantages of the interview style. But my aim is to make clear to an audience being introduced to them for the first time, some of the main ideas of three important philosophies. A little liveliness and a teasing taste of what they have to offer seems more appropriate in this context than a ponderous exegesis. But what I hope to convey most is a sense of how alive these ideas still are; and if it seems that I sometimes treat my distinguished interviewees with something less than old-world deference, the point is always to bring out these ideas, together with their limitations, and display something of the personalities behind them.

"The idea I have never ceased to develop is that in the end you are always responsible for what is made of you. Even if you can do nothing else besides assume this responsibility. I believe that a man can always make something out of what is made of him. This is freedom. . . ."

Interview with Sartre, 1970 [*New Left Review*, London)

1   *Jean-Paul Sartre*

1905–1980

April 15, 1980. Jean-Paul Sartre died today. Or was it yesterday? It is hard to tell from the initial press release. But it doesn't really matter; the greatest philosopher of our time is dead.

"I do not believe it," he wrote twenty years ago in *France Observateur,* upon hearing of the sudden death of his one-time friend, Albert Camus. Now it is our turn not to believe, despite the fact that Sartre's death followed a decade of blindness and ill health. I never met him and yet, it is as if I knew him, as if he were always there reminding us of our responsibilities, jabbing us with his teasing humor, impressing us with our own importance, puncturing our easy pretentions—the true Socratic gadfly.

"Death haunts me at the heart of my projects," he wrote in the early 1940s; and yet, he added, "it is always beyond me." And indeed, it was. Sartre criticized his former mentor, Martin Heidegger, for his gloomy emphasis on the importance of death for life; for Sartre, the emphasis was wholly on life, on "existence," and his writings have been badly characterized, by those who have not enjoyed them, as themselves "gloomy" and ridden with anxiety and loneliness. But Sartre was nothing if not playful—even about death. *No Exit (Huis Clos)* is a play set in hell, a black comedy with the dead as its characters; along with the seriousness, Sartre was always the comic. He considered himself the great optimist, declaring one day in the mid-1960s that he had never been unhappy in his life.

Sartre captured the term "existentialism" so thoroughly that others who might have applied it to themselves, indeed, who had influenced him in his use of it—such as Camus and Heidegger—felt forced to reject it in order to avoid being lost in his shadow. And if existentialism is one of the few philosophies to survive its fashionable phase in Paris, that too has been due to the genius and the persistence of Sartre, who, by speaking only to a select group of initiates and addressing topics that escaped the masses, never allowed himself to become a cult figure. He was always accessible; he saw himself as the spokesman for the workers of the world, who no doubt rarely read him. Like Socrates, who used his wit and his convictions to keep difficult issues alive and put an end to easy complacency, Sartre was a philosopher of the streets. His political opinions were often mistaken, sometimes downright foolish. But he always exemplified his own philosophy: that one must be "engaged" and committed, and avoid scrupulously a posture of "waiting to see what will happen." Perhaps, despite his brilliance with words, he never fully understood the media and the dynamics of public opinion; for example, when he did not condemn some young German terrorists outright but admitted that he at least understood their frustration, it was widely assumed that he supported them. He always insisted on calling himself a marxist—a label which in America at least, is too easily interpreted in exactly the wrong manner—as if its bearer rejected individual freedom, had nothing but praise for Soviet society, and accepted the totalitarian features of Russian communism.

But the watchwords of Sartre's philosophy, from the 1930s to the present, have always been *freedom* and *responsibility*. The key to Sartre's thought is that every individual must choose and act for himself or herself. He insisted that we are always responsible for what we do, no matter what the ready excuses or the circumstances. He always rejected what he called "vulgar" marxism, which denied individual choice and responsibility and hence a place at the very center of history, and which sought to replace individual responsibility with abstract forces over which society has no control. And if this philosophy seems like a "burden" or a "predicament," as so many authors have concluded, or as "gloomy" and "full of despair," as the popular press likes to declare, it is only so to those who prefer to excuse themselves—deceive themselves, Sartre would say—into thinking that they as individuals do not count, that they are mere pawns of the universe. But there is nothing necessarily "gloomy" about self-acceptance and the sense of taking one's life in one's own hands.

Sartre wanted nothing less than to change humanity through his writings. From his German mentors—Hegel, Marx and Heidegger —he learned his global perspective with all of its complexities and traumas. But at his philosophical heart he was totally French, and his ultimate model was René Descartes, that paradigm of clarity and reason, that champion of freedom—in particular, freedom of mind. It is mind that distinguishes being human from everything else; and we can imagine, we can dream, we can scheme—virtually anything. And it is in this confrontation between our imaginative consciousness and the obstinate resistance of the world that Sartre's existentialism was born. To change the world, to try to, to reject those who say "we can't," to encourage those who think that we can—that was Jean-Paul Sartre's philosophy.

He wrote of Camus: "He represented in this century, and against history, the present heir of that long line of moralists whose works perhaps constitute what is most original in French letters." We can now say that of Sartre too.

"A man is nothing else but the sum of his actions," he wrote in 1947, "he is nothing but what his life is." But he was wrong about that; Sartre was always more than the sum of his actions, even more than his life. For us, he remains what it means to be a philosopher, and, perhaps, what it means to be human.

The call came suddenly, as if in a dream. "Monsieur Sartre will see you now." Although I could not determine the direction of the voice, the enormity of my excitement overshadowed my confusion. Shortly, a very distinguished if hungry-looking gentleman in formal dress appeared and led me down a seemingly endless corridor to an anonymous white door. Without a smile or a gesture, he opened that door as if to show me, rather than introduce me to, a small and fragile man smoking a heavy pipe and wearing thick glasses, whom I immediately recognized to be Sartre. His age was indeterminable, and, in any case, the person before me seemed more a parody of Sartre than a flesh-and-blood human being—rather a projection of what I thought of him and what he thought of himself. His eyesight, in death, had evidently been partially restored, for while he was seated at a small café table, a half-finished carafe of wine before him, he had apparently been reading various newspapers from around the world, in which his death had just been reported. A large mirror behind him dominated the room. A clock ticked loudly on the mantle, and the unexpected but distinct sound of crickets was discernible—although there were no windows in the room. "Here he *is*," announced the valet, with a note of dry humor. Sartre obviously caught the irony, and looked at the man askance with his good eye. "Yes, I *am*," he responded cooly, "at least until you and the others have decided what to do with me." I wasn't sure whether the latter part of this remark had been addressed to the valet or some more authoritative voice, or—the thought occurred to me—to me. But, in any case, the valet bowed slightly and, with a bit of a smirk—barely detectable—backed out the door.

SARTRE: You are surprised they allowed you to see me, I suspect.

RCS: I certainly am, especially now that you're . . . gone.

SARTRE: Dead, you mean. But death is nothing, and so it makes no difference.

RCS: But according to your own philosophy, sir, it would seem to make *all* the difference.

SARTRE: Yes, that's why it makes no difference at all. I am—or was—my life, and nothing else. Jean-Paul Sartre is now, as I once wrote about Proust, nothing more than his works.

RCS: But surely there is something more than that: your plans and ambitions, the people you influenced, the enormous impact you have had on all thinking people in the twentieth century— even those who have never really read you. . . .

SARTRE: My plans and ambitions are no more; only the works themselves live. And they are for the most part unread—or misunderstood. Most of the people whom I influenced would have been so influenced without me, and my "impact," as you call it, is a creation of the press. I was merely an excuse, except to myself and a circle of friends. I do not believe in being admired; I do not want to be an institution.

RCS: Is that why you turned down the Nobel Prize for literature in 1964?

SARTRE: Yes.

RCS: But you are an institution, you know that, don't you?

SARTRE: I do not care.

RCS: But how do you react to these obituaries? For example, this one, which calls you "existentialist giant," or this one, "a modern Don Quixote"?

SARTRE: But that is not *I;* that is a fabrication which for the rest of history will bear the name "Jean-Paul Sartre, 1905–1980." The stories will change, and "Jean-Paul Sartre, 1905–1980" will change along with them. I have never believed in obituaries, although I've written some. No one can confer meaning on another, at least not without reducing him or her to a mere thing, an object with such and such characteristics, which in the case of myself is utterly irrelevant, at least to me.

RCS: Perhaps I can go back and set the record straight.

SARTRE: No, I am nothing, and there is nothing to tell.

RCS: But you want them to get it right, don't you, sir?

SARTRE: It makes no difference.

RCS: I can go back with my notes of our conversation.

SARTRE: You will see that no one will believe you.

RCS: I can describe you to them.

SARTRE: Go ahead, describe me to me.

RCS: Well, you're . . . I guess I can't. You seem to change as I look at you.

SARTRE: Indeed, you should see what happens when I look at myself, in the mirror over there, for example.

RCS: I thought . . . well, in your play, *No Exit* . . . you make a great point of insisting that there are no mirrors in Hell, no way of seeing ourselves, and therefore we are at the mercy of others and their opinions. "Hell is other people," you wrote in *No Exit,* and seemed to prove it.

SARTRE: Ha, ha, yes. That was one of the many things I believed back then. Incredible, isn't it, that I actually believed that?

RCS: That there were no mirrors in Hell, you mean?

SARTRE: No, no. Besides, we're not exactly in Hell here, you know. I mean the idea that self-reflection is the touchstone of self-recognition, and other people are obstacles—distorting mirrors, as it were.

RCS: In *No Exit,* I remember that the young coquette Estelle, who is wholly absorbed in her looks, is desperate for a mirror, and even wonders whether she exists without one.

SARTRE: Yes, and in desperation she pleads with the others to look at her. I have changed my mind about that; "they" gave me the mirror in this place out of spite, no doubt. They've read everything, you know, and carefully—as if to impress on me daily that my reflection, whether in the mirror or in my mind, is of no significance at all. And that which is of significance, perhaps all that is of any importance, is the reality of other people.

RCS: So Hell is not other people?

SARTRE: No, Hell is not other people.

RCS: Well then, why did they let me see you here in Hell?

SARTRE: I told you, we are not in Hell . . . because you don't matter at all. My friends, of course, they count for everything. And a handful of readers in Paris, many of whom I've lost in one way or another. If only I could be with them now. But you . . . you're just a phantom yourself, one of those hundreds of people who write books and articles about me and my work and have the senseless idea that you are somehow connected to me. But you're not, and so you make no difference at all. Thus, they have let you see me in order to tease me. For you, this is an interview with a celebrity, a unique opportunity; for me, it is absurd. Tedious too, if there weren't all the time in the world to kill.

RCS: You mean, *out* of the world. But whom would you like to see?

SARTRE: Simone[1] of course. François Jeanson. And, if it were possible, my one-time friends, Maurice Merleau-Ponty, Paul Nizan,[2] and Albert Camus. [*looks upward, dreamily*] We had such good times together, in the old days. [*getting angry with himself*] And inevitably split apart because of our differences. What a waste! The friendships were always what counted.

RCS: Camus?

SARTRE: He was, perhaps, my last good friend.

RCS: Why did you break?

SARTRE: I? No, it was he. He was always mad at me for something, something I said, something I wrote, something I didn't write . . . a good fellow, however.

RCS: And Simone de Beauvoir?

SARTRE: Simone? She has been the other half of my life, of course, much more than a friend; my essence, perhaps.

RCS: You seem to have changed your mind quite considerably from the forties, from the "Hell is other people" philosophy of *No Exit* and the "Relations with others is essentially CONFLICT" of *Being and Nothingness*.

SARTRE: Yes, I change, or rather *changed*, my mind quite often. Each time I was quite certain I was correct; but later, I would see that I was only one-half or one-quarter right. Incredible, isn't it? But mainly, amusing. [*muses to himself, chuckling*]

RCS: I'm surprised to find you so jolly. That is certainly not the person I expected to find here.

1. Simone de Beauvoir, one of France's leading novelists and essayists, was Sartre's companion for fifty years. Her works include *The Second Sex; Force of Circumstances; The Mandarins;* and *Memoirs of a Dutiful Daughter*.

2. Maurice Merleau–Ponty was a friend of Sartre's from college and, second only to Sartre, the leading philosopher in France until his death in 1961. He coedited *Les Temps Modernes* with Sartre and wrote some of the most important works in the phenemenological movement in France, particularly *Phenomenology of Perception,* which was written at the same time as Sartre's *Being and Nothingness,* with which it has many affinities.
Paul Nizan, another college classmate of Sartre's, was the most politically active of the group and a committed member of the Communist party. Nizan was killed in World War II, but Sartre considered him a victim of the tension between his own idealistic marxist principles and the vulgar marxists of the establishment left. He was the model for the character Brunet in Sartre's trilogy, *Roads to Freedom*.
Francois Jeanson remains Sartre's most loyal disciple in Paris. It was his review of Camus' *The Rebel* in Sartre's journal that triggered the ultimate break between Camus and Sartre. Jeanson often provided the bridge between Sartre's philosophy and his radical politics. His work *Le Problème Moral et la Pensée de Sartre* was published in 1947.

SARTRE: You mean, because I'm here? Oh, you mean because my philosophy is so full of desperation and hopelessness? [*laughs*] Look at this. [*picks up a newspaper and reads, in passable English:*] " . . . his view of the human condition as angst-ridden and despairing." Or this one, " . . . man as a responsible but lonely being, burdened with the terrifying freedom of choice." Ha, ha, ha.

RCS: Not so?

SARTRE: I have never been in despair, and I have never imagined despair as an emotion that could ever belong to me. Even here. [*looks around the room, fixes his glare at his reflection in the mirror, sticks out his tongue and giggles.*]

RCS: But your philosophy—?

SARTRE: I know. In the 1940s, and for obvious reasons, despair was all the fashion in Paris. We all paid homage to it in our writings: Camus, obviously, with his concept of The Absurd; Malraux; [*pauses*] all of us.

RCS: So what do you think "the human condition" really is, now that you've been through it?

SARTRE: "Been through it?" Oh, goodness, my boy, no one ever "goes through it." We each have our taste of it, and that's enough. But this "human condition"—where did you hear about that?

RCS: From you, I thought.

SARTRE: [*chuckling, lighting his pipe*] Yes, yes, I suppose I did believe in something like that. Funny how it changes every time my philosophy changes. And every time the world changes. No, the human condition—the "essence of man," you might call it—is another fabrication, like your idea of me as "Jean-Paul Sartre, 1905–1980." We create it as we go, all of us. But there's no such thing. And if there is a "condition humaine" it certainly would not be anxiety.

RCS: What might it be?

SARTRE: History, time, the fact that we are thrown into situations not of our choosing, that we must make our own condition, making history on the way.

RCS: One of your followers who is popular in America, Rollo May, has called our time "the Age of Anxiety." How do you feel about that? Could your philosophy have been true for its time?

SARTRE: "True for its time"? What does that mean? In 1940, I wrote that "Whatever the circumstances, and whatever the site, a man is always free to choose . . . '' When I read this, I say to myself, "That's incredible! I actually believed that!" But it wasn't any more true then than it is now. And that's the case with "the Age of Anxiety" as well.

RCS: So you've changed your view of freedom too?

SARTRE: Changed it? Well [*momentarily serious*], I don't know that I have. I've come to grips with it. Times have changed. The "either–or" choices we faced during the war have been replaced by much more real and complex choices about how to create a society worth living in for everyone. But I would say freedom is still the central concern of my entire philosophy, the freedom one has. The responsibility for what one is, even if there has been little that one could have done about it. The responsibility for what one makes of what is made of one, perhaps. But, no, I haven't changed my mind about freedom and responsibility.

RCS: "Man makes himself."

SARTRE: I still believe that simple-minded little slogan.

RCS: "Man makes himself"; but you just said that sometimes one can't help what is made of oneself.

SARTRE: No, I said one is still responsible for what one makes of what is made of oneself. There is always that glimmer of freedom, the possibility that one will refuse to give back that which his conditioning has made of him and expects him to return, the possibility of saying "no!" even when all else is lost.

RCS: Freedom is just another word for nothing left to lose?

SARTRE: Freedom is everything to lose. And now I've lost it.

RCS: But you seem free enough here. They leave you alone. They give you newspapers . . .

SARTRE: But nothing, you notice, with which to write.

RCS: I'd be delighted to leave you my pen and some paper.

SARTRE: It wouldn't do any good. Look. [*snatches* RCS's *pad and pen, which* RCS *is already extending to him. He writes, but the lines disappear.*]

RCS: But you're free to think, at least.

SARTRE: Free to think? What is that worth? By itself, I mean. I have always considered thinking to be an adjunct of writing; in fact, I can't really think unless I am writing. The purpose of writing is to get your cause across to other people, to cajole them, to convince them, at least to arouse them. What would Socrates have done if he could only have written notes to himself, instead of arguing in the public square?

RCS: I don't know.

SARTRE: Of course you don't! He couldn't have done anything. He wouldn't have been Socrates. Writing is my way of reaching people, of engaging the world. Thinking is merely the prelude to action. And here there's no action. No people. No conflicts. No causes.

RCS: You could fight with me. Convince me of something.

SARTRE: [*laughs*] No, you don't count. They thought of that.

RCS: Thanks a lot.

SARTRE: Don't be offended. You think you know me, but I'm just the bug you study in your library to find something to write about. And why? What are you trying to change? What is the *point* of your writing?

RCS: Uh, well, I don't know. Well, to try to get people to understand your writings.

SARTRE: As I said, you don't count.

RCS: [*speechless*]

SARTRE: But I don't want to discourage you. This is an original project you have here, and the first interview I've had since I died. So go ahead, ask me anything you want.

RCS: Anything?

SARTRE: It doesn't matter.

RCS: Why are you here?

SARTRE: What do you mean? Oh, for example, what was my crime? You don't seem to understand the situation here. It's not Heaven if you're good and Hell if you're bad, with someplace in between until "they" decide. No. This is nothing more than the echo of life, turned into a joke, that is, if you have a sense of humor. If you don't, it's torture. But it's not a question of good or bad, reward and punishment. I've committed no crime. I've no regrets . . .

RCS: *No* regrets?

SARTRE: No regrets. I'm content with everything—the way in which I lived my life, that is. What would be the point in feeling any other way?

RCS: What is that clock doing over there? I thought there could be no time here.

SARTRE: Perhaps you would be pleased with a clock with no hands?

RCS: Er, yes, it did occur to me.

SARTRE: My life hasn't been that much of a cliché, has it?

RCS: No, but . . . that clock seems to be keeping perfect time.

SARTRE: Indeed it is, or maybe it is. Anyway, I wouldn't know how to check. But that isn't the point. The clock is there for me to make of it what I will. I can watch the time passing, think of the infinity of moments yet to come, or contemplate what must be happening among the living, or ignore it as one of the pointless peculiarities of this most unpeculiar room. Time doesn't mean anything, in itself.

RCS: It's what we make of it.

SARTRE: And as there's nothing for me to do, there's nothing to make of it.

RCS: I guess that makes sense.

SARTRE: Certainly it does.

RCS: O.K. What are the crickets in the background? I came here through some labyrinthine hallway, and yet, the feeling I have in here is that we're out in the countryside somewhere.

SARTRE: Yes, yes [laughs a little]. I have always despised the country. The banality of nature. It is the intercourse of men and women that I love, the life in the city. So, of couse, they gave me crickets.

RCS: Pretty diabolical!

SARTRE: Not at all. I wouldn't have done it differently myself.

RCS: Can I ask you about your philosophy?

SARTRE: You mean, the philosophy of "Jean-Paul Sartre, 1905–1980"?

RCS: Yes, that's the fellow.

SARTRE: Well, I'm not sure I know much more about it than many other people who would have been much easier to interview, but go ahead.

RCS: Do you still consider *Being and Nothingness* to be your most important book?

SARTRE: What *I* consider is irrelevant. Those who like to make me an "existentialist" will certainly think so.

RCS: Aren't you an existentialist?

SARTRE: I? I'm nothing.

RCS: [*a little exasperated*] I mean Jean-Paul Sartre (1905–1980).

SARTRE: I'm sure he has no objection to that.

RCS: [*frustrated silence*]

SARTRE: During the later years of my life, I saw mainly the flaws in that book, and so I moved on, sometimes as if the book did not exist. If you had asked me that question in 1960, I would have said my *Critique of Dialectical Reason*, which cost me my health, among other things. But if you had asked me at almost any other time, I would have said that my most important work was the one I was working on, or had just completed. I can give you an answer, however: my novel *Nausea,* which I wrote in 1938. I still think it is the best thing I ever wrote. A couple of plays, *No Exit* and perhaps *The Devil and the Good Lord.* My two large philosophical works, but especially the *Critique of Dialectical Reason.* I would be happy to be remembered for those. That would be enough.

RCS: Why did you never follow up *Being and Nothingness?*

SARTRE: Ah, but I did. See, that is why these retrospective "interpretations" of my work will never give you even Jean-Paul Sartre (1905–1980); I wrote a long treatise that I never published, which means that even the experts don't know all my work. I'm certain you will see it soon. No doubt someone has unearthed my manuscript—since I never threw things away—and will publish it as a new wealth of insights into "what JPS *really* meant."

RCS: There's a second volume of the *Critique* too, isn't there?

SARTRE: Yes, that was about to see the light.

RCS: Will these two new works change what we think of your philosophy?

SARTRE: That depends on what you think my philosophy is.

RCS: Well, I know you won't like this, but . . .

SARTRE: Oh, I like just about everything these days.

RCS: Let me go through your writings and your career with you. O.K.?

SARTRE: "O.K."

RCS: Your childhood. You have said that you were without friends, but you thought yourself a genius. Your great uncle was Albert Schweitzer, who won the Nobel peace prize in 1952. You were raised without a father and consequently, or so you said, "without a superego." You were raised by women, and so have always preferred their company.

SARTRE: Yes, but you left out the most important element in the childhood of Jean-Paul Sartre (1905–1980): *words.*

RCS: Oh yes, *The Words.*[3]

SARTRE: I never liked my body; in fact, I have always been ugly as a toad. I distrusted authority, but I generally obeyed. I was cynical about religion, even with a great Christian in my family, and I was extremely naïve about, and later shocked at my own unwitting complicity in, politics. So I came to trust one thing, the quintessence of things—words. Words have always been my *metier,* my way of meeting people, relating to them, my way of defining myself, my way of taking hold of things, my hold on the world.

RCS: But as a student, as a philosopher, you became a phenomenologist, that is, one of those philosophers who sought to have direct contact with "the things themselves" as Husserl put it.[4]

SARTRE: Yes, I was initially a "phenomenologist," if you like. *Being and Nothingness* is certainly a very phenomenological book.

RCS: It is subtitled "An Essay in Phenomenological Ontology."

SARTRE: But that already shows you that it was not just a piece of phenomenology, for Husserl always tried to insist that phenomenology is not ontology.

RCS: Just a moment, Monsieur Sartre. What is phenomenology? What is ontology?

SARTRE: It is quite simple, really: Husserl defined phenomenology as the study of the essential structures of consciousness. Ontology is the study of beings, a theory about the basic things in the world that make up "reality." Now what I did—and I was guided by one of Husserl's own pupils, Martin Heidegger—was to say that one could not do phenomenology without doing ontology, too. It is impossible to treat consciousness as if it were some free-floating realm detachable from the world. To understand the one meant to understand the other. I have always been a realist, but without sacrificing consciousness to the reality of mere things.

RCS: You mean, without denying that consciousness is real?

SARTRE: Yes—consciousness confronting the brute existence of the world—that was my philosophy then.

RCS: I have always admired one passage of your work, perhaps

3. Sartre's autobiography, trans. Bernard Frechtman (New York: Braziller, 1964).

4. Edmund Husserl (1859–1938), Czech-German philosopher and founder of the phenomenological movement.

more than any other. It is where you apply this so-called phenomenological method in your novel *Nausea*. I see you have all your books here; could I ask you to read it to me?

SARTRE: "They" put the books here. But certainly, I have no objection to entertaining you. I take it that you mean the encounter with the chestnut tree. [*pulls the book off the shelf, separates a couple of pages and reads:*]

> I was in the park just now. The roots of the chestnut tree were sunk in the ground just under my bench. I couldn't remember it was a root any more. The words had vanished and with them the significance of things, their methods of use, and the feeble points of reference which men have traced on alone in front of this black, knotty mass entirely beastly, which frightened me. Then I had this vision.
>
> It left me breathless. Never, until these last few days, had I understood the meaning of "existence." . . . It is there, around us, in us, it *is* us, you can't say two words without mentioning it, but you can never touch it. . . . Even when I looked at things, I was miles from dreaming that they existed: they looked like scenery to me. I picked them up in my hands, they served me as tools, I foresaw their resistance. But that all happened on the surface. If anyone had asked me what existence was, I would have answered in good faith, that it was nothing, simply an empty form which was added to external things without changing anything in their nature. And then, all of a sudden, there it was, clear as day: existence had suddenly unveiled itself. It had lost the harmless look of an abstract category: it was the very paste of things, this root was kneaded into existence . . . this hard and compact skin of a sea lion, . . . this oily, callous, headstrong look. This root, with its colour, shape, its congealed movement, was . . . below all explanation. . . . To exist is simply to be there. . . .

RCS: Terrifying. Now what does that mean?

SARTRE: What do you think it means?.

RCS: That consciousness confronts existence and is repulsed by it; that the abstract categories of the mind are not—as many philosophers seem to think—the basis of reality.

SARTRE: Not bad. Yes, the central theme of that whole part of my career—which I think you might call quite rightly the

phenomenological phase rather than the existentialist phase—
was characterized by a basic duality: consciousness on the one
side, brute existence on the other. Both are real, and neither is
reducible to the other.

RCS: Sounds very Cartesian.

SARTRE: But of course. Every French boy learns Descartes' basic
philosophy, with its fundamental split between mind and body
and the centrality of the "I, " while still in grade school. I was no
different, and it always remained my ontological model.

RCS: Despite your reading of Heidegger and Kant and other German philosophers?

SARTRE: Yes.

RCS: And this then provides the theme for *Being and
Nothingness?*

SARTRE: Yes, but you're jumping ahead of the story. In 1936,
before I wrote *Nausea* and almost five years before *Being and
Nothingness,* I published an essay called "The Transcendence of
the Ego." It was a basic exercise in phenomenological description, and my main point was to show that an adequate description of consciousness did not disclose, as both Descartes and
Husserl thought it would, an "ego," a "self," an "I."

RCS: I think you said, "My 'I' is out there in the world, like the
'I's' of other people."

SARTRE: Yes, the point being that the self is not something ex-
perienced as such, but only, as I argued later, something that we
create through our actions. But this changes the nature of that
dualism between consciousness and brute physical existence.
Consciousness is not "I," it is not *self*-consciousness, or much
less, as Descartes thought, something that can be translated
"I think, therefore I am." Consciousness is much more than
thinking, but much less than an "I." In fact, consciousness is
empty; it has no contents; it is only that activity, that tendency—
like a wind blowing from nowhere—toward everything in the
world.

RCS: I'm not sure I see the distinction. Can you give me an example of consciousness without an 'I' in it?

SARTRE: Certainly. When you are running after a streetcar, you
are not conscious of the thought, "Here I am, running after this
streetcar." Or at least, it would be very odd if you were. What
you are conscious of is the phenomenon of "the-streetcar-to-be-
overtaken." The "I" does not appear until later; for example, if
you become embarassed.

RCS: So "the transcendence of the ego" means that the self is not *in* consciousness but rather a potential object of experience, reflected back at us in the world?

SARTRE: Yes. Consciousness never catches itself in the act, so to speak; it is always ahead of itself and always escapes our scrutiny. I try to catch myself thinking *now*—but the "now" is already gone, and I'm only trying to remember. The passage you asked me to read in *La Nausea* is the other side of that duality; whereas consciousness is essentially ephemeral, empty; physical existence, on the other hand, is full, a "plenum," a brute presence which confronts us whether we like it or not.

RCS: And the self?

SARTRE: It stands uncomfortably in the middle, not quite existing, but not nothing, either.

RCS: Thus your title, *Being and Nothingness—L'etre et Le Neant.*

SARTRE: Yes, the "le neant" (nothingness) is consciousness, and I take that quite literally. Consciousness is not a possible object of consciousness and so it is nothing. But also, it is through consciousness that negation comes into the world; it is only according to our demands and in line with our expectations that something is absent, or changed, or destroyed. Otherwise, the world just exists, one way or another. Thus, Descartes could doubt everything, even the existence of the world; and a terrorist can plan the destruction of everything. Being simply *is*: it is *what* it is; it is *as* it is; it just *is*. But the ideas of destruction and reconstruction, seeing the world as it is not, as it could be otherwise—those are the products of consciousness. And the being through whom nothingness comes into the world must itself be nothing.

RCS: But the fact that it is nothing also means that it has no "essence," right? Because it is not "something", it can't be something in particular.

SARTRE: Right! Consciousness itself cannot be fat or stupid or shy or friendly or cowardly or old. But you're jumping ahead of the game. Let's establish the basic ontology first.

RCS: All right.

SARTRE: Now I distinguish two kinds of being—although this may sound paradoxical at first: being-*in-itself* (en-soi), the brute existence of things, and being-*for-itself* (pour-soi), the existence of consciousness. This is, as you have commented, quite thoroughly Cartesian. I define being-in-itself simply as being *as* it is, *what* it is, simply *being*—like the chestnut root in the park. But being-for-itself I define in terms of negation, as nothing—or to use one of my favorite paradoxes, it is what it is not, and it is not whatever it is. Being-for-itself, unlike beings-in-themselves, is not yet anything at all. Being-for-itself has the power of *transcendence*.

RCS: You used the same word a moment ago to describe the fact that the self was outside of consciousness. Now I'm confused.

SARTRE: What I mean by transcendence is the ability to imagine alternative possibilities, to plan ahead, to formulate projects and ambitions, to create oneself. Thus, the "transcendence" of the self. It is a project, a possibility, rather than a thing to be found already in consciousness. And we create our selves not by looking inward but by acting, by changing the world.

RCS: But mere things can change the world, too. A tornado, for example. Does the tornado thereby create a self?

SARTRE: No. A tornado moves things around, breaks them apart, of course, but it is only through human consciousness that one arrangement rather than another *means* anything.

RCS: So transcendence is essentially a property of consciousness, because things have meaning only to a being that is conscious?

SARTRE: Yes—this is why I say, again following Heidegger, that things, beings-in-themselves, don't have transcendence, don't have what Heidegger calls "possibilities." They can't project themselves into the future. They can't have conscious *projects*.

RCS: So consciousness is quite essential to your view of human existence?

SARTRE: Of course.

RCS: And this is the same as saying that consciousness is simply freedom?

SARTRE: Yes and no. That is the formulation that is provided by Kant, for instance, and in a simpler version by Descartes. I too want to say that consciousness is essentially freedom; this is why I am so adamant in insisting that it is nothing, because that means that it cannot be anything determinate, or anything determined by anything else. But I do not want to say, as Descartes and Kant seem to have believed, that there is a realm of human consciousness that is distinct from nature, immune from the causal laws of nature, and a kingdom unto itself.

RCS: You say, "consciousness *is* freedom"; why don't you just say "consciousness is free" or "man is free"?

SARTRE: It is a device that I borrowed from Kant; it is a way of *protecting* freedom. If you say simply "consciousness has freedom, as one of its properties," then it is possible to suggest other properties that are more important, or to find excuses why, in some particular case, one wasn't really free—because of an emotion, or an illness, or some particularly pressing set of circumstances. But by insisting that consciousness itself *is* freedom—an awkward way of putting it, I admit—these excuses are blocked. There are no conditions for freedom, and no ways of cancelling it—except, of course, obliterating consciousness itself.

RCS: But how can you have both—the view that consciousness is essentially freedom, and the view that consciousness is not apart from the determinacy of nature in general? Do you believe in the general causal determinism of nature, that every event has its sufficient natural causes?

SARTRE: Of course I do. I have never said and have never believed that consciousness is an ontological exception to the laws of nature. That again is why I insist on saying it is nothing. But insofar as it is something—that is, insofar as we find ourselves filled with desires, inculcated values, motives and emotions, insofar as I have this body and exist in this place and at this time—we are, I am, indeed determined. My thesis is rather this: as we said earlier of the clock here ticking away on the wall, the important consideration is what we are to *make* of these things. For nothing is wholly determined in our experience. Everything, even the direst emergency, is presented for our consideration as an opportunity, never as a causally complete determinate factor, such as a coiled spring in a watch, or the instinctual mechanism in a bird building its nest or flying south for the winter.

RCS: You say you are a determinist?

SARTRE: I do.

RCS: And you believe that every event has its natural causes?

SARTRE: Yes.

RCS: And yet you insist that all human actions are free, that we are always responsible for what we do, even when we seem to have no alternatives?

SARTRE: That bothers you? Well, in fact, it is in part an old argument of Kant's: that the question of freedom is not a question of the lack of causal determination. I agree with him that the very suggestion is nonsense. The question of freedom is a question of subjectivity, a question of how the subject must see his own situation.

RCS: Give me an example, please.

SARTRE: Certainly. Suppose that we are reliving the Resistance, and that one of our friends is a known coward, a man who has panicked in every action of any intensity in his entire life. He knows it. His friends know it. It is agreed by all that he is a coward, and he says so himself. But now the chips are down, and for various reasons a vital and dangerous action must be entrusted only to him. There is no other workable option. Now, let us say that he thinks about this, reflects on his history and on what he and everyone else consider to be his "character"—that is, one of a coward—and he says to himself, "I am going to panic. I am going to fail. I have always done so. My character causes this to be so. And I will always do so." What will happen? Well, of course, he is going to panic. It is as if he has already set himself to it. But now suppose he steels himself in the following manner: He looks at his past; he reflects on his cowardice, and he vows this time to succeed. His friends are doubtful; we expect the worst. But he does not listen to us. He insists and, perhaps, he succeeds. But the point is not whether he does succeed. The point is that, even if we were to suppose that there is something "in him," some determinate quality which makes him act as a coward, this is not for him to acknowledge. For his acknowledgement is thereby also an act of resignation: in effect, a decision that there is no use trying to act otherwise. His freedom to choose, in other words, has nothing to do with what he in fact will do. One can choose the most hopeless of causes, and in doing so, one proves oneself free.

RCS: But can you generalize that example? Is that true of ordinary human activities as well?

SARTRE: Of course. Giving up smoking, for example. Whether in fact one *can* do it is not the question of freedom. It is rather a question of *will*.

RCS: But now it sounds as if freedom is nothing but having a certain intention.

SARTRE: But one cannot have an intention without trying to act on it, and thereby acting. The assassin whose rifle jams at the crucial moment, in one sense does no more than move his finger; but he has acted no less than if he had succeeded. Success does not depend on one's freedom alone, and freedom does not depend on success.

RCS: Then what does it mean to be free?

SARTRE: I think that the best account of my view of freedom was in my book about Jean Genet, a petty criminal but a master writer. Genet was *made* a thief by the people around him, while he was still a child. These "good citizens" did not directly make him steal, of course, but when they found the young urchin taking some things, they called him a "thief." He accepted the description and became a thief. It is a tiny change, from the imposition to the acceptance, but this tiny change, was the beginning of a long process in which Jean Genet became both thief and poet, both an exile from and in the limelight of society. His is not a happy freedom, to be sure, but it *is* freedom; he marked out in increments a road in life which was not, at any stage, given to him. But in retrospect, of course, one can always look back and say, "Ah, we knew he would end up this way all along; it could not have been different." And one can always find evidence to show why this is so. But retrospect is not the domain of freedom, and on the road to freedom, things might always be different. At least, we cannot help but believe that they might be.

RCS: But do you not defend a doctrine that you call "absolute freedom," at least in *Being and Nothingness*?

SARTRE: Ah, yes. I've since given that up as too extreme, but I still believe in the basic idea of it: that consciousness always has that small if infinitesimal gap between itself and pure being; that one is *never* in a position of utter helplessness; that we are never mere pawns of forces beyond our control. Perhaps it is merely a question of perspective, always insisting on the question "what can I do?" or, after the fact, "what could I have done?"

RCS: Don't you believe that we do things beyond our control, compelled, for example, by unknown desires or repressed fantasies?

SARTRE: That is, of course, an important question, the question of "the Unconscious." But you have to remember that I was raised in the land of Descartes, believing in the crystalline transparency of consciousness and the immediate, even infallible, knowledge we have of our own states of mind. Freud was virtually an undiscussed figure in France until only a few years ago, when suddenly a number of Frenchmen began to behave as if they had invented him. But the Unconscious in the land of Descartes, that was blasphemy. So, no, I did not give any credence to the idea that there were hidden forces in the mind itself which, unbeknownst to us, determined our every move and desire. I rejected and I still reject the *mythology* of the Unconscious that psychoanalysts use to explain human behavior. I reject their attempt to reduce all relationships to a single primal relationship, and I especially reject what I call the mechanistic cramp in Freud's own description of his theory, the biological and physiological language he uses, and words such as "repression" and "instinct." But having said this, I hope you will also recognize that although I am in complete agreement with the *facts* of repression and disguise, I do not describe them in that manner. In fact, the whole of *Being and Nothingness* is, in one sense, a diagnosis of the various ways in which we hide our own intentions and decisions from ourselves. But it is something *we* do, not a mechanism inside of us. But I totally agree with Freud that what we hide from ourselves can trap us and limit our freedom.

RCS: In emotions, for example?

SARTRE: Yes, emotions, in particular, are often (but not always) traps which we set for ourselves with our own freedom of mind. You may not know this, but I wrote a book in 1937-or-so on the mind, one part of which has been published as *The Emotions: Sketch of a Theory,* in which I argue that our emotions are "magical transformations of the world": in effect, actions of just such a kind. They are a subtle form of escape behavior, ways of coping with the obstinacy of the world by avoiding it. But we pretend that they "happen to us" and force us to do this or that, when indeed they are rather our strategies for preventing action, avoiding situations.

RCS: For example?

SARTRE: Do you know Aesop's fable about the fox and the grapes? I'm certain that you do. The fox lusted after the grapes but could not, however he tried, get them in reach. And so he concluded that they must be sour. Now the grapes didn't change their chemistry. He changed them by his view of them. That is what I mean by "a magical transformation of the world." And it is a method of avoiding responsibility.

RCS: So you do believe in the unconscious?

SARTRE: NO. I do not and cannot make any sense of what you call "the unconscious." What I do know is that people often conveniently ignore their own decisions and their own activities, sometimes under the guise of "forgetting" but usually by simply ignoring them. All those behaviors that are attributed by Freudians to the mysterious forces of the unexplorable "Unconscious" can be explained thereby.

RCS: It sounds as if we have reached one of your major themes. You have said repeatedly that freedom and responsibility were your most enduring commitments, but what about the *avoidance* of responsibility? The *denial* of freedom?

SARTRE: Of course; that is what I call "bad faith" or *mauvaise foi,* to deny what one is—or is not. We do it all the time. In fact, I have sometimes suggested that we cannot help but be in bad faith, that it is as much a part of human nature as the demand for freedom itself.

RCS: "Human nature"?

SARTRE: Well, yes, in a manner of speaking. You might say that the essence of being human is to be free, which means not to have an essence. But let's not dwell on this kind of paradox now. The point is rather that human existence revolves around one enormous complexity, which perhaps I can best present in traditional philosophical form. I have already cited my allegiance to Descartes and his division of everything (apart from God) into being–in–itself (of things) and being–for–itself (of consciousness). Well, I also said that being–for–itself has one all-important aspect, which I call transcendence—the ability to envision oneself as something other than one is, to see things as other than they are.

RCS: And that is what you call freedom.

SARTRE: Yes, but the obvious fact about all human existence is that it is not *only* this, for the ability to make oneself other than what one already is presumes that one already *is* something. And this starting point, which for every one of us seems so astonishing, so outrageous, so . . . coincidental, is just as much a part of us as our transcendence.

RCS: For example?

SARTRE: Well, the fact that I was born with my particular face and body; the fact that I was born in Paris of white, European parents. The fact that I was born in this century, as opposed to any other. And this totality of facts about me I call (I borrowed the term from Heidegger) my *facticity.*

RCS: Facticity is then opposed to transcendence?

SARTRE: No. It complements transcendence. There are no facts about us that are beyond our overcoming, albeit often at considerable cost. And there is no imaginable change that is not grounded in the way in which we already are—our race, our class, our age, our education.

RCS: But if we can change anything, what is left as a brute "fact" about us? The year of one's birth? One's height?

SARTRE: Not even such things as those. One can take great pains to lie about one's birth, hide the facts and create the appearance of new ones.

RCS: But one doesn't change the fact of one's birth date.

SARTRE: No matter; it is what one makes of it that counts, a matter of pride, a matter of embarrassment, an utter irrelevancy, a point of controversy.

RCS: And your height?

SARTRE: Haven't you noticed how some very tall men slouch a lot, as if to hide their height? And do you know about the artist Toulouse–Lautrec who compensated for his dwarfish appearance by acting every inch the dominating giant around Paris?

RCS: Then how do you know what the difference is, between those aspects of you that are given as facts—your facticity—and those aspects which are open to change—your transcendence?

SARTRE: You cannot know.

RCS: Oh!

SARTRE: And that is how bad faith becomes so essential. Bad faith, to be more precise, is a denial of either one's facticity or one's transcendence.

RCS: How is that?

SARTRE: Well, some cases of bad faith are easy to spot. For example, in *Being and Nothingness* I gave the example of a waiter in a café. His movement is a little too precise. He is a bit too eager, his voice and expression a bit too solicitous. When he takes an order, and when he turns to the bar, there is that inflexible stiffness, like some kind of automaton, as he carries his tray with the control of a tight-rope walker, forever avoiding loss of balance by the masterful movements of his arm and hand. It is as if his movements were mechanisms, as if he were playing a game. But what game? We need not watch long before we can see that he is playing at *being* a waiter in a café.

RCS: I can see that you long for those cafés.

SARTRE: Yes, but let me stick to the example. The condition is one of ceremony. It is an obligation of all tradesmen. The grocer is expected to act like a grocer, a tailor like a tailor. Each is expected to deny his transcendence for the convenience and comfort of his customers. But if these examples seem innocent enough, consider the soldier who acts as he is expected to act—as a military machine—a soldier-*thing,* who obeys his orders without a murmur, who does what he does as part of his *function.* Then you can see the horror of bad faith; men who deny their ability to choose—even if the only alternative is death—by pretending that they are things, by acting as if they were pure facticity. That is bad faith. That is the negative role of my existentialism.

RCS: It is a concept, like your example of the soldier, that was evidently given a powerful impetus by your heroic experiences in the war and in occupied Paris.

SARTRE: Oh, my own experiences were nothing heroic, but, yes, you are right. Like most of my ideas, this one was formulated and received its importance from that particular situation.

RCS: And after the war?

SARTRE: I was still sensitive to bad faith, but in more subtle areas—anti-Semitism and racism, for example. The anti-Semite, for instance, turns the Jew into a thing in order to deny his own faults, and to blame someone else for his failures. The anti-Semite is a man who is afraid—not of the Jew, of course, but of himself—of his conscience, of his instincts, of his responsibilities, of solitude, of change, of society, and of the world, of everything *except* the Jews. Thus he chooses himself as a person, with the permanence and the impenetrability of a rock, the total irresponsibility of the warrior who obeys his leaders—and he has no leader. The Jew is only the pretext for his bad faith; if he were elsewhere he would be equally prejudiced against blacks or Orientals. Anti-Semitism, in a word, is fear of one's fate.

RCS: In some of your more recent writings, you seem to indicate that bad faith isn't so much a universal human condition as a condition of the bourgeoisie.

SARTRE: Let me be careful here. In my early works, *Nausea,* for instance, the bourgeoisie I despise is the fat and complacent majority of most middle-class societies, for example, those in provincial France or suburban America. Now, I use the term more as Marx did, to signify an economic class—the rich, basically. But in both cases, there is a philosophical pretention to be attacked—namely, that the interests of the bourgeoisie are the interests of humanity in general. And I should say that *Being and Nothingness,* in my opinion now, is bourgeois in this sense also: I claimed to express the essence of being human, but in fact express primarily the concerns of a middle-class Parisian intellectual in 1940.

RCS: I want to go back to something you said a while ago, about the essential human dilemma. You said that bad faith is the denial of transcendence and the retreat into facticity, or vice versa. Then you gave the examples of the waiter and the soldier. But some time ago you suggested to me that there was no way in which to know one's facticity from one's transcendence. Isn't this an essential incoherence in your theory?

SARTRE: No. It is rather an essential ambiguity in human existence. Consider, for example, any of those features of a personality that psychologists so matter-of-factly label "traits": shyness, or cowardness, or friendliness. They look like facts, and to so accept them is to indeed make them into facts, to make them true. But their actual function is as excuses: [*falsetto voice*] "Oh I can't do that, I'm too shy." But the explanation is precisely the opposite of what the situation involves: one does not refuse to do something because of shyness; one excuses one's decision not to do something by becoming shy. And so too with cowardice, or friendliness, or any other human trait.

RCS: So you are saying that many of the so-called "psychological facts" about us are actually excuses, decisions, and thus part of our transcendence.

SARTRE: Yes, but it works the other way around too. In one of my first novels, *The Age of Reason,* I invented a character called Mathieu, who obviously resembled me in many ways. He was a 37-year-old philosophy professor (I wrote the novel in the mid-1940s) who had a professional commitment to be free. That is, he *talked* about freedom all of the time. He refused to marry the girl with whom he had more or less been living for years, and whom he had just made pregnant, all "in order to preserve his freedom." He did not join his friends in the civil war in Spain, "in order to keep his options open." But he was, as his older and very bourgeois brother pointed out to him, in total conformity with all of the institutions he claimed to despise and reject. He too was in bad faith, but in an opposite manner from our waiter–machine and soldier–thing; he pretended to be all freedom, all transcendence, refusing to acknowledge how he was restricted by the facts of his life.

RCS: Is there a middle way, a kind of balance, in which one can avoid bad faith?

SARTRE: I do not know whether one can be both wholly engaged in an activity and sufficiently aware at the same time. I do know that every time I was sufficiently removed from one of my own opinions or activities to look it squarely in the face, I could see that I had been guilty of bad faith too.

RCS: Is that what you are going through now?

SARTRE: Essentially, but with a sense of humor that only death makes possible. And that makes all the difference.

RCS: One thing you haven't mentioned at all, and that surprises me, is God. You don't believe in God?

SARTRE: You know very well that I do not. But not out of any bitterness. I just do not believe "by instinct" as Nietzsche once said.

RCS: But don't you argue in *Being and Nothingness* that man wants to be God, and that this is his tragedy?

SARTRE: Did I say that? Incredible! Well, yes, everyone wants to be God, but what I mean by that is an argument that you will find in the hardly radical writings of the scholastics of the thirteenth century. Each of us consists of both facticity and transcendence, as I've said, and bad faith emerges from both the tendency to think of oneself as all facticity—as if one could identify with the list of credentials on a job application form—and the tendency to wish oneself totally free—as if by some magical stroke we could become somebody else, perhaps by joining some exotic religious cult, or throwing oneself into a new love affair. But if you take both of these tendencies at once, what do you get? A wish to be totally in–itself and for–itself at once, all possibility without restriction, and yet something secure, given, permanent, eternal. And this, of course, was just how some of the medieval philosophers defined God. And they even said—as did St. Thomas Aquinas, for instance—that man wanted to be like this, too, and therein lies his longing for the divine. Well, I guess that I believe that too, except that I don't see it as a tragedy. It's just the way things are.

RCS: But it doesn't mean that you believe in God?

SARTRE: No. It means that I believe that God is an impossibility.

RCS: And that is why man is without a purpose? Without an essence?

SARTRE: What!

RCS: You know, the argument you presented in 1947 in your lecture "Existentialism is a Humanism," that a paper knife or cookie cutter has a function because it is designed to serve a certain purpose, but, because there is no God, we do not have any such purpose, or any predetermined "human nature."

SARTRE: Did I say that? Incredible! Well, the argument is obviously fallacious; whether or not there is a human nature depends on something more than God's intentions. But more important, you shouldn't take that lecture too seriously. It was a mistake, an attempt at popularization that didn't come off.

RCS: It was the most widely read of your works.

SARTRE: Oh my God! . . . Sorry. Oh well, too bad. No, my arguments about the nature of human existence have virtually nothing to do with the question of whether there is or is not a

God. If there were a God, the arguments would be precisely the same. And if there is not . . . no matter.

RCS: Do you still believe that now?

SARTRE: Of course. I haven't changed my mind about everything.

RCS: You know, it has often been commented how Christian your philosophy is, despite your atheism. The concept of inescapable bad faith, for instance, has often been linked to the concept of original sin; your emphasis on action and will with the Lutheran doctrines of good works and conscience; and your equation of virtue with the continual overcoming of temptation.

SARTRE: And why should that worry me? I have also been called a dogmatic marxist by the conservatives, a traitor and a revisionist by the marxists, a puritan by the libertines and a libertine by the moralists. I don't really care what people say about me.

RCS: Ah, but didn't you say that you had retracted your old philosophy of the autonomous, isolated individual, in favor of a new emphasis on the importance of other people?

SARTRE: Yes, but not other people in general, such as readers I've never met and people who know me only from the newspapers. I do think that virtually everything in my consciousness was effected by and mostly created with other people, but that doesn't mean that I have to explain myself to every clown and critic who thinks that existentialism is a fine tune to dance to.

RCS: Let me ask you about your views of other people, and how they have been changed. In *Being and Nothingness* you argued that the essence of our relations with other people is *conflict*. Is that not right?

SARTRE: Right that I said it, wrong as a thesis.

RCS: And there you argued that "being-for-others" was a third ontological category, along with being-in-itself and being-for-itself, right?

SARTRE: Yes, but I also insisted that it was ontologically on a par with the other two, and not derivative from them.

RCS: Nevertheless, it is introduced several hundred pages along in the book.

SARTRE: That's true. I clearly saw relationships as secondary—or as a threat—to individual consciousness.

RCS: And you must admit that the very title "being-*for*-others," as opposed to "being-*with*-others," for example, is already a little paranoid. It sounds as if you see yourself at the mercy of other people, rather than seeing them as friends, companions, playmates, and so on.

SARTRE: Yes, but that was what we were thinking in those days. Think of Camus' *Stranger,* for instance, in which an innocent, solitary man is destroyed by those around him. In the days of the Resistance, we naturally suspected everyone—felt at their mercy. In my own examples, I discuss that draining experience in which one's solitude is interrupted by the intrusion of another person, as if the landscape is sucked into the sinkhole of the other person's consciousness. And, my favorite example, the awkward instance in which I am peering through a keyhole—I do not say exactly at what—and someone else arrives on the landing; *the look (le regard)* of the other throws me into a paroxysm of self-consciousness, and I am no longer aware of what I was looking at before, but now only of myself, being *looked at.* We *are* at the mercy of other people. They have the power to make us into what we are.

RCS: And that is where the self arises?

SARTRE: I do not see it quite that way now, but yes, that is where one finds the origin of self-consciousness, not in the solitude of Cartesian self-reflection, but in the reflection of others.

RCS: An embarrassing source of self-consciousness.

SARTRE: In English, of course, "self-conscious" means precisely that—"embarrassed."

RCS: That's true, but that, surely, is not all there is to selfhood.

SARTRE: I never said so. It is just one of those existential traumas that continuously reminds us of ourselves.

RCS: The distinction between an occasional existential trauma and the nature of human existence doesn't always come through clearly in your writings.

SARTRE: It doesn't usually come through clearly in life either.

RCS: There is one question we keep avoiding, the one you called "paradox" a few moments ago. Is there such a thing as "human nature" or "human essence"? With your famous slogan of 1947, "existence precedes essence," you argue that we create our essences. I know you have dismissed that lecture as a "mistake," but I am not clear about what you do believe.

SARTRE: I have always believed that there is something essential to man, because man is conscious, and that is *freedom.* If you like, to be free is human nature, not, mind you, simply the desire to be free, but *being* free. But to say that man is free is to say that many of the motives and drives by which philosophers and other theorists have tried to define human nature—for example, the idea that people are basically selfish, or that everyone needs to be loved, or that we are "naturally" social animals, or rational animals, or anything else—must be viewed as options and choices, not as necessities.

RCS: So you do not believe that any specific characteristics, apart from freedom, can characterize humanity in general?

SARTRE: Well, yes and no. There are no given characteristics, in the form of determinate drives, instincts or motives, which make it necessary for people to act this way or become that. We are not, in a sense, a part of nature, as Descartes argued too; we have given up the guarantees that other creatures, from cockroaches to cattle, obtain from nature regarding what they are to do. But there is one argument in that lecture which I still find enormously convincing: the idea that, just as one creates his own character through the acts he performs, so he also contributes to the creation of the character of humanity as a whole by being an example, by making it true, at least in this one case, that humanity is capable of selfless heroism, or utter selfishness.

RCS: Is that like Kant's imperative, "act so that the principle of your action can be universalized as a law for all men"?

SARTRE: It is related to Kant, except that he thinks the principles precede the act and are already rational; that is, if they are worth doing. I do not believe in such rational principles but rather insist that one creates one's principles in acting; in the beginning is the act, not the word, not the principle. And that means that one has no assurances that what one does is "right"; one does it, that's all. One sets an example and hopes that the world will follow.

RCS: Your own political commitments, which have been much in the news for many years now, have hardly been followed by the world. Indeed, you've repudiated many of them yourself, in retrospect.

SARTRE: "In retrospect" again; it is so easy. But at the time all I know is what seems to be the right course of action. And so I act, even if my action is nothing more heroic than handing out hand-bills on a street in central Paris, surrounded by the press and television and providing coverage for a workers' movement which would otherwise be ignored.

RCS: How do you know it is the "right" course?

SARTRE: I don't, in one sense; but I obviously follow a rule of thumb in such matters: that it is always the most radical alternative, the farthest to the left—that will be the "right" one. Even if, later on, it turns out that it was not as it seemed.

RCS: Isn't that fairly dogmatic? What of all the arguments of the intellectuals on the right? Don't you even listen to them?

SARTRE: There *are* no intellectuals on the right. Functionaries of the bourgeoisie, perhaps. Practical theoreticians. But an intellectual stands for the universal, for humanity, even though his roots and even his personal interests are wholly on the side of a particular class or social group.

RCS: Can one stand for what you call "the universal"?

SARTRE: Obviously, I have believed so for the last decades of my life. As a student, and even when I was writing *Being and Nothingness,* I was oblivious to my own class interests, and I thought—or pretended—that I was writing for all humanity. I found out that I was wrong, but I did not change my ambition, only the class on behalf of which I was writing. And I agree with Marx, of course, that the only universal class is the working class, the "proletariat," for their interests will not be served until there are no classes at all.

RCS: This is obviously not the place to argue politics with you, M. Sartre, but let me at least ask you to comment on what you have said you consider your most important book, *The Critique of Dialectical Reason,* which came out in 1960.

SARTRE: Yes, I nearly killed myself writing that book—too many amphetamines, too little sleep—but I felt an urgency, not so much for myself but for the book itself. It was my corrective to *Being and Nothingness;* and it was my ultimate attack on the communists.

RCS: Weren't you yourself a communist?

SARTRE: Every French intellectual flirts with the Party, but I have always kept my distance from them, and they have always despised me. In fact, my existentialism was at one time branded "ideological public enemy no. 1." I have often shared their opinions about international politics, that is, when they were not merely toadying to the USSR, but my philosophy has always been incompatible with their vulgar materialism and their reduction of men to mere cogs in the dialectic. My marxism, and Marx's too, begins with a theory of individual freedom. "Man makes history," Marx wrote, and communism has ignored him ever since.

RCS: But the *Critique* itself is about marxism.

SARTRE: No, it is not *about* marxism; it *is* marxism. And in it I try to prove that marxism and existentialism are not incompatible, but rather, properly understood, they presuppose one another.

RCS: How does the *Critique* differ from *Being and Nothingness?*
How does it correct it?

SARTRE: Well, to begin with, *Being and Nothingness* was about
individuals, about consciousness and contact between individuals. The *Critique* is about society, about groups. In fact, it
is more of a work in sociology than what you would probably
consider philosophy.

RCS: Some critics have contended that the book loses sight of the
individual altogether.

SARTRE: But it is not a book about individuals. I did not mean
for the *Critique* to replace *Being and Nothingness,* but to correct
its one-sidedness and to complement it.

RCS: How does it do that?

SARTRE: In *Being and Nothingness,* I said much too little about
how individuals are molded and affected by the large and largely
static institutions that make up society, or what I call the
"practico-inert." And that is what the *Critique* is about. And in
Being and Nothingness I considered man as mainly a consciousness with a body, but I worried almost exclusively about the
demands of consciousness. In the *Critique,* I worry more about
the needs of the body, and the basic questions of economics.

RCS: What about freedom?

SARTRE: Freedom is still there, at the very core of the theory, of
course. I should add that, with my usual propensity for exaggera-
tion, I sometimes insist that, insofar as man is victim of his own
institutions and inequities, he is a slave and not free at all. But
don't take that too seriously. It is still freedom that is the course
of everything, and one of my main arguments in the *Critique* is
against the common tendency to treat groups and societies as
organic units, with individuals merely as "members."

RCS: And you disagree with that?

SARTRE: Fundamentally. Groups are not organisms but tenuous
collectives of individuals, sometimes but not always held
together by a common past and shared interests (the "practico-
inert" again), but always liable to disintegration. Most
sociologists worry about the structures of groups; I am more
concerned with their formation and disintegration, and that
comes back, once again, to a matter of individual freedom.

RCS: What do you mean by "dialectical reason"?

SARTRE: Very simple. "Analytical reason" is trying to understand something by watching it, or dissecting it; "dialectical

reason" is understanding through participation, by being part of what you are trying to understand.

RCS: You prefer dialectical reason?

SARTRE: In all matters concerning human conduct, yes.

RCS: "Dialectic" is what you used to call "engagement."

SARTRE: In a sense, but "dialectic" is also a bit more aware than I was of history and the limitations of the individual.

RCS: You have a reputation for having encouraged violence in politics; was that true?

SARTRE: You sound shocked. But violence is not always the worst alternative, and to eschew violence on principle is to let others have their way by violence, and thus be their accomplice. Do you remember the speech in my play *Dirty Hands:* "How frightened you are of dirtying your hands. Oh well, stay pure! What good will it do anyone and why did you join us? Purity is a monk's ideal. You intellectuals and bourgeois anarchists, you make it an excuse for doing nothing. Do nothing, then. Wear gloves, but as for me, I've got dirty hands, dirty up to the elbows."

RCS: How would you describe your politics?

SARTRE: My politics? I've always been an anarchist.

[*The valet steps quickly through the door. He says nothing, but waits for* RCS *to join him.*]

RCS: M. Sartre, this has been the dream of my life.

SARTRE: Indeed, that is all it has been.

RCS: I was always so certain that you would be dogmatic and authoritative and impossible to talk to.

SARTRE: [*chuckles*] I was, but it no longer matters what I say. My conversation with you was like looking into a mirror.

RCS: You mean . . .

SARTRE: No. I mean only that, ultimately, perhaps, it does not matter with whom one speaks, that what one always finds is another human being, like oneself.

RCS: I cannot accept that; talking to you has been a rare and special experience.

SARTRE: Perhaps, then, you still have something to learn. But not from me.

"Philosophy is essentially untimely; it can never find an immediate echo in the present. When such an echo seems to occur, when a philosophy becomes fashionable, either it is no real philosophy or it has been misinterpreted and misused for ephemeral and extraneous purposes. . . . But what is useless can still be a force, perhaps the only real force. . . . What is untimely will have its own times."

—from *The Fundamental Question of Metaphysics*

2

Martin Heidegger

1889–1978

It is a beautiful sunny day in June 1947. I—a young and brash American philosophy student—cannot quite believe that I have just been talking to (conducted an interview with, yet!) the legendary Martin Heidegger. We met in a tiny beerplatz near the University of Freiburg. It was one of those stand-up bars that was intended to fit a dozen people, but there were at least fifty or so squeezed between an old piano, a half dozen rustic tables, and the bar. It was so noisy that we could barely hear one another, which seemed not to bother him. I have tried to record our conversation as faithfully as possible, but I am sure you will see that I did not always understand what Professor Heidegger said. And yet, as one reads through the transcript of the interview from beginning to end, I think a fairly definite sense of his philosophy emerges, even if nothing seemed all that clear at the time.

Why Professor Heidegger agreed to grant me the interview is a matter of some curiosity. He has refused interviews with many famous philosophers and has consistently shunned the press. For many years he and his wife have lived in virtual seclusion in the Black Forest region of southern Germany. He is not often seen in public, except for his occasional lectures in the city—either here or in Heidelberg—which inevitably draw a hard-packed standing-room–only crowd of thousands. In such a circus, I am told, it is almost impossible to understand what he says, if indeed one can hear it at all; but the audience is always transfixed and appreciative, as if graced with an invitation to some great world-historical event. In fact, Heidegger's devotees here seem to regard him more as a prophet than as a philosopher in the ordinary sense. I have heard him described as the only spokesman for salvation in our post-theological, obsessively technological age. I have heard that he has complained, à la Nietzsche, that "in two thousand years, we have not invented a single new god." And, judging from his own language, it is Heidegger who intends to give us one.

Personally, I find these claims excessive. I have tried to read Professor Heidegger's monumental book, *Sein und Zeit* (*Being and Time*), published twenty years ago, in 1927. I admit that I understood very little of it, but I should say too that I always had a sense of something, some profound insight which, as the following interview will make embarrassingly clear, I still am incapable of explaining to you. Yet, I feel as if I agree with him, even if I can't tell you what it is with which I agree. Strange. Perhaps that is Heidegger's power, but it must be something more as well. When I met him, I found him overly stiff and formal, but at the same time unrefined and gruff. Despite the fact that there were only the two of us, I sometimes felt that I was being lectured to like an entire class of freshmen, and I walked away after several hours with the sense that I had not really *met* anyone. He was wholly devoid of anything that could be called "charm," and yet he had an aura of fascination that continued to draw me toward him.

Heidegger was once a student of the German-Czech "phenomenologist" Edmund Husserl (1859–1938). He was probably Husserl's most brilliant student (depending on whom you ask), although he fell out of favor when he disagreed with his teacher's most central doctrines. Husserl began by defining "phenomenology" as the study of the essential structures of human consciousness. Heidegger rejected the very notion of "human consciousness." Husserl was concerned with knowledge; Heidegger was far more concerned with the practical and emotional aspects of human existence; with issues of life and death; with anxiety, despair and care and concern. Husserl appealed to the eternal truths of mathematics; Heidegger was obsessed with history and historical change. Husserl urged precision; Heidegger preferred to look to the romantic poets of Germany and the more obscure philosophers of pre-Socratic Greece. And yet, from the first pages of *Being and Time,* it is clear that Heidegger thought of himself as Husserl's pupil, as a "phenomenologist" whose business it was to describe the essential structures of human experience, breaking away from all philosophical theories and established traditions in order to see for himself, in Husserl's famous words, "the things themselves."

Heidegger had a brush with the Nazis in 1933. Husserl, a Jew, was dismissed from the University, and Heidegger, publically separating himself from his teacher, was given the rectorship of the University. He resigned the following year, rejecting his brief enthusiasm for National Socialism, but the bitterness lingered on. It has often been suggested, though rarely well argued, that his philosophy led him to or allowed him to flirt with fascism; but the fact is that there is very little in the philosophy itself that would lead to that judgment. Indeed, Heidegger has always said that he has no moral theory, no ethical views, nothing to condone the Nazis, although perhaps not enough to condemn them either. In truth, as far as I can tell, Heidegger's philosophy is compatible with virtually anything, any style of life, any political views. But the moral indignation that still surrounds his flirtation with and the perfunctory speeches he made as Rector for nazism have turned many readers away from him, or at least provided them with a ready excuse for avoiding his very difficult prose. In any case, Heidegger was always an extreme national chauvinist, who loved uniforms, parades, and power. One doesn't need either his philosophy or sinister motives to explain his fascination with the Third Reich.

Is Heidegger an existentialist? Certainly it was he, as much as anyone, who brought the word "existential" into our philosophical vocabulary; who inspired Jean-Paul Sartre and the French existentialists in their explorations of the nature of human existence; who first said that our "essence is our *existenz,* " that "the essence of truth is freedom," that the human condition begins by "being thrown and abandoned into the world," that death is the most important fact about human life, and that anguish (*angst*) is basic to human nature. And again it was Heidegger, in *Being and Time* (written in 1927, fifteen years before Sartre's *Being and Nothingness*), who insisted that the purpose of life is "authenticity"—finding one's "true" self. In far more complicated language than Sartre's simple "man makes himself," Heidegger too insisted that man is "that entity which in its being has this very being as an issue," which can "choose itself and win itself or lose itself and never win itself." And yet, just this year (1947), he published his "Letter on Humanism," in which he repudiates both existentialism and humanism. That made my first question quite easy:

RCS: Herr Professor Heidegger, why do you not consider yourself an "existentialist"?

HEIDEGGER: For me *existenz* is that kind of Being toward which *Dasein* can comport itself in one way or another, whereas for M. Sartre and his friends it is merely one of *Dasein*'s ontical "affairs," not "existential" and not ontological at all.

RCS: Uh . . . ummm. What does "ontical" mean?
(There followed a long dissertation by Heidegger which I failed to record and did not understand. The noise was overwhelming.)

RCS: Well, um, Herr Professor Heidegger, you do know that *Sein und Zeit* is often considered a very "existentialist" book, and a major influence on M. Sartre and his friends.

HEIDEGGER: What you are calling an "influence" seems to me to be a major misunderstanding of my work. My project in *Sein und Zeit* was metaphysics, to raise once again the question of Being, a question which has fallen into oblivion. Being or *Sein* cannot be comprehended as any mere beings (*Seiendes*) and cannot be deduced from any higher concepts or represented by any lower ones. We are asking for the ground of Being, the essence of beings, that it is and what it is, and why it is rather than nothing.

RCS: Herr Professor Heidegger, I'm . . . not sure that I follow you. In fact, I haven't understood a word that you have said.

HEIDEGGER: Let me explain my position in this manner: M. Sartre and his existentialism are primarly an ethical philosophy. I have no ethical theories. I am not a moralist. And I think that almost everything that has been done in the name of "ethics," and by men fishing in troubled waters of "totalities" and "values," is fundamentally mistaken, an attempt to say what cannot be said.

RCS: That sounds very much like the philosophy of Ludwig Wittgenstein, Herr Professor Heidegger.

HEIDEGGER: [*haughtily*] I never read him.

RCS: Oh. Well, you have read M. Sartre, yes?

HEIDEGGER: Yes, I have some acquaintance with M. Sartre's philosophy. In my opinion, it is *dreck,* and you may quote me. As I have told you, I do not see any resemblance between the two of us. M. Sartre believes in values and I do not. M. Sartre totally ignores the question of Being. And I, assuredly, do not. In fact, M. Sartre seems not to understand the importance of *history* at all; perhaps he should read some Marx.

RCS: Herr Heidegger, could I ask you to explain this "question of Being"? What do you mean by this?

HEIDEGGER: I can ask, "How stands it with being"? or else, "Why is there something rather than nothing"? I can ask, "What are we saying of a being when we say that it exists"? and this is an entirely different matter than our asking about *existenz,* which is peculiar to *Dasein.*

RCS: Excuse me, Professor, can I slow you down for a moment . . .

HEIDEGGER: I don't have much time.

RCS: What do you mean? That only we humans exist?

HEIDEGGER: I didn't say "human"; I never do. No, of course one can speak with the vulgar, as M. Sartre does, and ascribe mere existence to everything that is, but for *Dasein* to exist is to call its Being into question, and that is its *existenz.*

RCS: Er, um, let me ask you a simple–minded question—actually a lot of simple–minded questions—sort of common sense questions . . .

HEIDEGGER: Philosophy has very little to do with common sense, and common sense has certainly proved itself indifferent to philosophy; it is blind to the things that philosophy sees before her essence-seeking eyes.

RCS: Yes, well, what is it for a thing to have existence?

HEIDEGGER: A thing. Yes.

RCS: What is it for a thing to have Being?

HEIDEGGER: Ah, but how can a thing *have* Being? Rather Being perhaps has a thing? Or rather, Being "has" us.

RCS: I'm feeling rather stupid, Professor Heidegger. Let me try it this way . . .

HEIDEGGER: Try what what way?

RCS: Um, the "question of Being," I guess. Are you asking, "What is the meaning of the word *Sein* (Being) in German (English)? Or are you asking the ontological question, what is the ground of being, which means, I guess, what must be true of a thing in order for it to exist? Or are you asking a kind of theological question, why is there Being rather than nothing at all? Which is rather like asking, why did God create the universe? Which of those are you asking, Professor?

HEIDEGGER: All of them. None of them. The word "Being" (*Sein*) is an enigma to us, spoken but not understood. And it is Being itself that interests me, not mere beings, which seem to so obsess M. Sartre. And you are right that my question, or rather, the question, is "rather theological" as you put it, but I do not ask why God created the universe. I do not know what it would be to ask such a question.

RCS: Oh.

HEIDEGGER: Anyone for whom the Bible is divine revelation and truth has the answer to the question "Why are there beings rather than nothing?" even before it is asked. Everything that exists, except God Himself, the increate creator, "is." But one who holds to such faith can only participate in our question by ceasing to be a believer and taking all the consequences of such a step. He will only be able to act "as if" . . .

RCS: Are you an atheist, sir?

HEIDEGGER: I do not find that an intelligible question.

RCS: Is Being for you the same as God?

HEIDEGGER: Being is the same as Being.

RCS: Nietzsche once said that concepts such as "Being" are "the last cloudy streak of evaporating Reality."

HEIDEGGER: Yes, I have quoted Nietzsche's remark. It is the guiding view of his entire philosophy, the fundamental support and . . .

RCS: May I buy you another beer, Professor?

HEIDEGGER: Yes, if you please. [*pause*]

HEIDEGGER: Now, where were we?

RCS: Well, I'd like to start over, if I may, Professor. I hope that you understand that we American philosophy students are enmeshed in what you call "common sense."

HEIDEGGER: That is why you have never had any philosophy.

RCS: Er, yes, I suppose. But I can ask you about some of the terminology that you have been using. It is unfamiliar to me.

HEIDEGGER: Yes, if you wish.

RCS: O.K. First, what is *Dasein*?

HEIDEGGER: You mean, *who* is *Dasein*?

RCS: Who is *Dasein*?

HEIDEGGER: *Dasein* is an entity that does not just occur among other entities, but is rather ontically distinguished by the fact that, in its very Being, that Being is an *issue* for it.

RCS: Does the word "ontically" just mean "by virtue of its existence"?

HEIDEGGER: Not *existenz,* but by virtue of the fact that it *is,* yes.

RCS: Then *Dasein* is a thing . . .

HEIDEGGER: An entity.

RCS: . . . an entity which thinks about its own existence—I mean Being—just by virtue of the fact that it happens to exist.

HEIDEGGER: Yes. But in this case, this is a constitutive state of *Dasein*'s Being, which implies that *Dasein,* in its Being, has a relationship toward a being—a relationship which is itself one of Being.

RCS: That is what you mean when you keep saying that we can understand Being only by first understanding the being through which Being is disclosed; that is, we have to understand ourselves in order to understand Being.

HEIDEGGER: Understanding of Being is itself a definite characteristic of *Dasein*'s Being. *Dasein* is ontically distinctive in that it *is* ontological.

RCS: O.K., that *Dasein* is "ontically distinctive" means that we are unique, as human beings, in that we are onto-*logical,* which means that we can ask questions about our own existence, about why we exist, and about what it means to exist, and so on.

HEIDEGGER: "Being ontological" is not yet tantmount to "developing an ontology," but, yes, we are ontically distinctive in that we can and must raise the question of Being.

RCS: So, what you are saying is that to be human is to question one's own existence, and . . .

HEIDEGGER: It is to grasp the question of Being.

RCS: . . . and to ask philosophical questions in general?

HEIDEGGER: Yes, although most philosophical questions are still "pre-ontological."

RCS: So to be *Dasein* is to be a human being?

HEIDEGGER: No, you have not understood what I have been saying. Do you think I coin new German words just for the hell of it? If I were talking about "human being" I would say "human being." I am talking about *Dasein*.

RCS: What is the difference between being human—being a person—and being *Dasein*?

HEIDEGGER: To talk about a difference would mean to compare two different entities, but we are not talking about two different entities.

RCS: You mean because *we* are *Dasein*.

HEIDEGGER: Yes.

RCS: *Dasein* simply means "being there," doesn't it? For example, if I asked you where your umbrella was, you could say, in colloquial German, *da/sein*?

HEIDEGGER: But I am not talking colloquial German, or common sense either. Nor do I see what my umbrella has to do with philosophy.

RCS: Nothing, sir, but do you mean by "being there" what you are referring to when you talk about our being "abandoned" in the world? Why not simply talk about being human, or perhaps being conscious, or am I misunderstanding you again?

HEIDEGGER: [*exasperated*] Let me begin again. You do know what phenomenology is, do you not?

RCS: Yes, sir. Or at least I think so, sir.

HEIDEGGER: Good. The phenomenon is a showing of itself, or rather, a showing of itself-in-itself. This is what my teacher Edmund Husserl meant when he talked about "the things themselves." A phenomenon is not a mere appearance. It is not an experience or an "idea" in our so-called minds. Do you understand this?

RCS: Yes, sir.

HEIDEGGER: Good. Now, if phenomenology is to ensure that we do not let ourselves be led astray by overhasty theories, but to experience things as they are, let us ask if, in our experience, we ever confront, as a phenomenon, ourselves as "human."

RCS: Aha, I see what you mean! What I experience is myself in the world. I discover that I'm human only by comparing myself with other entities, and seeing that I fit a certain category, but that isn't my immediate experience of myself. What I know of myself firsthand is only that I am conscious of the world.

HEIDEGGER: No, you do not experience being conscious either. What is this consciousness? You do not experience *it*. What you experience is the world, just being-in-the-world. That is all that you are, "in-the-world." What you are and who you are are questions of a very different sort.

RCS: So what I experience, firsthand, is just *being here*?

HEIDEGGER: Yes. *Dasein*. To say anything more would be to assume, without any warrant whatsoever, that you experience your being there as a particular kind of being, which you do not know except by what you are told by and in comparison to others. If we are to be phenomenologically precise, we must say that what we experience, first of all, is simply *Dasein,* not ourselves as consciousness, not ourselves as human, not indeed ourselves as anything in particular at all.

RCS: So that is why you say that *Dasein* is the Being whose Being is in question. At first I thought you were saying something much more trivial than this.

HEIDEGGER: I never say anything trivial.

RCS: I can see that. So *Dasein* isn't so much a technical term for something quite specific, but rather an intentionally open-ended term that refuses to make presuppositions about what we are.

HEIDEGGER: Yes.

RCS: Thus, when we describe the essential structures of consciousness—I mean *Dasein*—it is an open question whether we are describing just the features of our own minds—I mean *Dasein*—or the universal features of all human consciousness—all human *daseins*—or the features of all *daseins*.

HEIDEGGER: We are describing the essential features of *Dasein*.

RCS: And what that is—that is, what we are—is an open question.

HEIDEGGER: Yes, we cannot define *Dasein*'s essence by citing a "what" of the kind that pertains to a subject matter. In addition, we cannot define it, because its essence lies rather in the fact that in each case it has its Being to be, and has it as its own.

RCS: And this is what you call *existenz.*

HEIDEGGER: Yes, this is what I call *existenz*—the possibilities of *Dasein* to itself, to be itself or not to be itself, whether it has chosen these possibilities itself or maneuvered itself into them or grown up in them.

RCS: Would you agree with Sartre that man makes himself?

HEIDEGGER: What? *I* should agree with Sartre?

RCS: Never mind. So "existential" means for you those aspects of *Dasein* which have to do with choosing oneself, with understanding one's "existenz" *ontologically*?

HEIDEGGER: One's mere existence is merely one of *Dasein*'s ontical "affairs," as I've said; it is the ontological structure of *existenz* that is essential.

RCS: But of course one has to exist in order to examine the nature of *existenz.*

HEIDEGGER: Of course, but to understand one's *existenz* is not just to know that one exists.

RCS: Like Descartes, for example, "I think therefore I am."

HEIDEGGER: Yes, that is an empty formality—not the discovery of *existenz* at all.

RCS: One thing bothers me: how much is choosing one's possibilities a matter of actually acting, really doing something to realize one's possibilities? And how much is it merely understanding, that is, becoming an existential philosopher?

HEIDEGGER: What do you mean, "merely understanding"? The essence of *Dasein*'s existenz *is* understanding.

RCS: Does this mean that our essence is not what we do?

HEIDEGGER: The essence of *Dasein* is *"to be."*

RCS: But to be *ontologically*?

HEIDEGGER: Yes, to raise the question of that Being which is, in each case, mine.

RCS: "In each case mine"; you mean for all of us?

HEIDEGGER: I didn't say that.

RCS: May I give you another beer, Professor?

HEIDEGGER: Very well.

RCS: You said that *Dasein* is "in each case mine." What do you mean?

HEIDEGGER: *Dasein* has to be in one way or another, and each of us has to make a decision about our ownmost possibilities. *Dasein* is in each case this possibility.

RCS: And this is where you introduce the idea of existing *authentically,* right? To choose what you are is to be authentic; to choose what you are not is to be inauthentic.

HEIDEGGER: To be authentic is to choose oneself and win oneself; to be inauthentic is to lose oneself, or to only seem to choose oneself. The word you are using, "authentic," is not mine, however. It has nothing to do with being sincere or being genuine, those peculiarly French virtues. *Eigentlich,* which is the word I use, means something more like "own-ness."

RCS: Like "being one's own man"?

HEIDEGGER: Yes. It is, quite literally, "finding oneself."

RCS: How could one not find oneself? Whom else would one find? [*laughs*]

HEIDEGGER: You think you made a little joke? Well, the truth of the matter is that most people do not find themselves, but rather someone else, who is precisely not themselves.

RCS: Whom do they find?

HEIDEGGER: They find *das Man*.

RCS: Who is that?

HEIDEGGER: Let me explain.

RCS: Let me get something to snack on.

HEIDEGGER: Some for me too, if you please.

[RCS *asks the bartender to bring some cheeses and sausage.*]

HEIDEGGER: Now, the whole of Western philosophy, at least since Plato, has been caught up in the idea of the individual subject, isolated from the world and distinct from other people, don't you agree?

RCS: Well, I can think of some exceptions, but—yes, it has been our central theme, especially since Descartes.

HEIDEGGER: Correct. It is in Descartes in particular that the division between the subject—or consciousness—and the object—the whole of the world, including his own body—becomes absolute. But what Descartes presumed was that his immediate experience was only his own ideas, his consciousness, and we have already shown that this is not so.

RCS: Is that why you insist on the notion of *Dasein* as Being-in-the-World, and not a consciousness confronting the world?

HEIDEGGER: That's correct. Descartes' discovery was an illusion. There is no consciousness to be discovered, only one's Being-in-the-World, and one cannot separate that expression into a conscious Being, on the one side, and the "external" world on the other.

RCS: I have heard that you consider it a scandal that no one has yet provided a refutation of scepticism and proved the existence of the external world.

HEIDEGGER: No! I have said quite to the contrary that I think it's a scandal that anyone can still ask such questions. There is no "external world," for there is no "inner" consciousness either; there is just "being there" (*Dasein*), or "Being-in-the-world."

RCS: O.K. I see that. But what does this have to do with a person not being himself or herself, but being someone else—what did you call it?

HEIDEGGER: *Das Man*.

RCS: *Das Man*?

HEIDEGGER: Just as Descartes erred in viewing himself as a subject isolated from the world, he erred too in viewing himself as a subject isolated from other subjects, as if our knowledge of other people is something added onto our knowledge of our own existence.

RCS: And you disagree with that?

HEIDEGGER: It is exactly the opposite; we can know nothing of our own existence except through other people. We do not recognize ourselves first and then come to terms with others; the others are already in us. They define us. They tell us who we are.

RCS: Our Selves?

HEIDEGGER: No. They tell us that we are not our Selves.

RCS: I don't understand.

HEIDEGGER: We talk about "the Others" as if that means everyone except me, but we are not merely "being there," *Dasein*, over and against the others, but "being-there-too," along with those from whom one does *not* distinguish oneself.

RCS: So one learns who he is through these others, through one's place in the family, in the community, in school, at work?

HEIDEGGER: Yes, one learns to think of oneself in terms of what I call "undifferentiated average everydayness." Not as anyone in particular, but just as the–one–who–is–now–taking–out–the-garbage, or the–one–who–is–just–about–to–buy–another–beer.

RCS: And that is *das Man*?

HEIDEGGER: In essence, yes. *Das Man* is another clever coinage of mine, turning another idiomatic expression in vulgar German into a philosophical profundity.

RCS: You mean "man" as in *man ist* or in English, "one" as in "one is"?

HEIDEGGER: Yes, "one," as in "no *one* in particular . . ."

RCS: Or like the "they" in "they say that . . ."

HEIDEGGER: Yes. If you ask, "Who said that? Tell me exactly," there is no answer, for no one in particular said it, just the "they," some persons or others.

RCS: And that is what it is to not be oneself, to be inauthentic, to simply be what "they" say that you are?

HEIDEGGER: Yes, that is what I call "fallenness," to "fall back" unthinkingly into the anonymous roles in which one was raised, or which have been otherwise thrust on you.

RCS: So how does one become authentic, and find one's true self?

HEIDEGGER: By not falling.

RCS: How do you prevent that?

HEIDEGGER: By resolution, by *resolving* firmly to be oneself and not to fall.

RCS: And who or what is oneself?

HEIDEGGER: The who that is in each case mine.

RCS: And how do I know which who is mine?

HEIDEGGER: Ah, you want me to give you an ethics. That is not my business. I am interested only in understanding the Being that is in each case mine as a way of understanding Being as such.

RCS: If you aren't giving us an ethics why do you use terms such as "authentic" and "inauthentic"?

HEIDEGGER: You mean "ownness" and "un-ownness". These are ontological structures, not values.

RCS: But isn't it better to be *eigentlich* than *ineigentlich*?

HEIDEGGER: It is more *eigentlich,* to be sure.

RCS: I can see why people have said that your philosophy allowed you to join the National Socialists. How do you respond to that?

HEIDEGGER: [*angrily*] I do not respond to that.

RCS: Let me buy another round of beer.

HEIDEGGER: Mmmmph!

RCS: [*cheerily*] Now you were saying that *Dasein* is first of all *das Man,* undifferentiated and simply part of a social world. Does that mean that we are initially all inauthentic?

HEIDEGGER: No. [*pauses*] I mean what I say when I call *das Man* "undifferentiated." He is not authentic, but neither is he inauthentic. What we call "the world" is not, as philosophers have often said, the totality of facts and objects. It is rather a world of tasks and equipment, jobs to be done for people and with people. Primordially and for the most part the existence of *Dasein* is wholly caught up in these average everyday tasks and "being with" others. Authenticity is not yet in question.

RCS: Is that why, in *Sein und Zeit,* you describe the world in terms of a tool shed, the world as "equipment," instead of as a world of things, and our selves as workers and craftsmen rather than philosophical speculators?

HEIDEGGER: Yes, I despise cold intellectual reflection. "Things" emerge only with reflection, with a certain luxury and a certain distance. We view a hammer merely as a hammer; it is only when we pick it up and examine it, for example, or when its head flies off its handle, or something goes wrong with it that we view it as a thing. Primarily, it is what we use to hammer with and it is not a "thing" at all.

RCS: And this is how it is with other people too?

HEIDEGGER: Yes; we do not originally see other people as "other," but as constitutive of the world in which we have tasks to do, as "being with" . . .

RCS: And how do we ever stop being merely "with" other people, defined by them as *das Man,* as "someone or other"? How do we ever become authentic, or for that matter, inauthentic?

HEIDEGGER: Do you remember what I just said about the hammer? That it is not first of all a thing but a tool that we use. It is only when we suspect that something has gone wrong with it that we stop using it and look at it as a thing. And then we can ask questions about it as a thing, questions which we would not have asked before.

RCS: Such as?

HEIDEGGER: How do we come to have hammers? How is this hammer different from that one? Should we fix it or throw it away?

RCS: O.K. What does this have to do with *das Man* and authenticity?

HEIDEGGER: It is when something goes wrong, so to speak, with one's average everyday tasks, and our relations with other people, and ourselves.

RCS: What goes wrong?

HEIDEGGER: We recognize death.

RCS: We what?

HEIDEGGER: We realize that each of us is going to die.

RCS: Oh. [*pauses*] Let me excuse myself for a minute please, professor.

HEIDEGGER: I notice that you choose to leave as soon as I bring up the subject of death.

RCS: Oh no, Professor, I just need to . . .

HEIDEGGER: It is the expected reaction. It is death above all else that is one's ownmost possibility, that makes each of us ourselves, that is the key to authenticity. Your reaction is what I call *angst*—or anxiety. It is anxiety—in the recognition of death —that prompts us—or should prompt us—to recognize authentic selfhood.

RCS: To die is to be authentic?

HEIDEGGER: No. To face death is to be authentic, to realize oneself as "Being-unto-Death."

RCS: But we all know that we are going to die.

HEIDEGGER: We know it as an abstraction, a syllogism that says, "All men are going to die; I am a man; therefore I am going to die." That is not the same thing as facing death. That is not the same thing as facing one's own death.

RCS: I think I know what you mean. A doctor–friend of mine who routinely faces other people's death, became ill for the first time in his life last month, and he told me that it was the first time he actually ever faced his own mortality.

HEIDEGGER: Few of us ever do, but there is no authenticity without it.

RCS: So death is the meaning of life.

HEIDEGGER: No, death forces us to realize the meaning of life.

RCS: It is the thought that I am going to die, in other words, that makes me reflect on the meaning of the everyday tasks that I perform and the significance of the relationships I have with other people.

HEIDEGGER: Yes, knowing that one has to die is the shock that forces us to be ontological.

RCS: And to see the meaninglessness of our everyday tasks and relationships.

HEIDEGGER: No. No! NO! Why do you assume that to be authentic requires some desperate rejections of ordinary life and some wild quixotic adventure? I have never said that. Ontology doesn't mean rejecting anything.

RCS: You mean that one could continue to be a good *bürgerlich* housewife or bureaucrat and still be authentic?

HEIDEGGER: Yes.

RCS: Then I'm not sure I see what one has to do to become authentic.

HEIDEGGER: "To do"? It is not a question of doing but being, being ontological, and that means facing up to one's own possibilities.

RCS: You mean death is a possibility? I thought it was a necessity . . .

HEIDEGGER: It is our most necessary possibility.

RCS: But why? Why single out death as the one "possibility," as you call it, that makes each of us ourselves?

HEIDEGGER: Because each of us must die his own death. No one can die for you. No one can die instead of you. Strictly speaking, no one can die with you. Each of us has to die his own death, alone and for ourselves.

RCS: I can only go to the bathroom by myself and for myself, too.

HEIDEGGER: [*indignantly*] You just prove my point, that as soon as we turn to the most serious subject you become vulgar.

RCS: Sorry, Professor. I guess I just don't see how the recognition that we are going to die makes so much difference in the way we live, particularly as you say that becoming authentic doesn't mean that we have to change our way of life at all.

HEIDEGGER: I didn't say that one doesn't change one's way of life; I did say that one must become resolute in the face of death, and that is a monumental change.

RCS: Then what is it to be inauthentic?

HEIDEGGER: Not to be resolute. To ignore the fact that one is going to die. To "fall back" into one's everyday tasks and the hurly–burly of one's social life and act as if time does not matter, as if all of this could go on forever. [*pauses*] But now I must excuse myself for a moment, too.

[Heidegger *leaves and returns a few minutes later.*]

HEIDEGGER: To cross this crowded room was a difficult task, indeed.

RCS: I know. Perhaps that is a good illustration of your thesis, that we experience the world first of all as instrumentality, in terms of tasks and obstacles, in which "things" appear only when they become *conspicuous,* or *obtrusive,* or *obstinate,* such as that sign that reads *Herren,* or that overturned table in the middle of the room.

HEIDEGGER: Ah, I see that you have read my *Sein un Zeit* after all. Yes, it is when our tasks break down and our tools malfunction or fail to be ready-at-hand that they become conspicuous; or they may become obtrusive when they get in our way; or obstinate, when they refuse to function as we want them to.

RCS: So, in a sense, you are attacking the entire history of philosophy, which seems to think that "things" are simply there before us, and we experience them just as is, instead of as tools and so on.

HEIDEGGER: Yes, I see the whole of Western metaphysics, from Plato to Nietzsche . . .

RCS: Nietzsche?

HEIDEGGER: Yes, especially Nietzsche—as a failure to understand what I call *presence.* Instead, they insist on this wrong-headed idea that Reality is something Other, a world of things that we *know* about, rather than simply a life that we live *in.*

RCS: Yet before Plato, you seem to indicate that the so-called "pre-Socratic" philosophers had it right. At least, you have recently spent an enormous amount of time interpreting their few remaining fragments.

HEIDEGGER: Yes, I believe that those premetaphysical thinkers— and they really were thinkers, understood—which is to say, felt at home in—the world in a way in which we surely do not. But at the same time, they did not have all our glib views of the world—and so they appreciated the *strangeness* of the world as well.

RCS: So what you called understanding (*Verstehen*) means "feeling at home"? That is a very romantic notion, isn't it? The poet Hölderlin, for example, whom you have studied, used to talk about that feeling, too.

HEIDEGGER: Yes, understanding is feeling at home in the world. It is not mere knowledge. It is accepting the place in which you are put. But neither is it the undifferentiated feeling at home of *das Man* and average everydayness. Perhaps I have not been insistent enough; thinking ontologically comes only with a great effort. And most of what we call "thinking" is not that at all. Indeed, the most thought-provoking thing about our age is that we still are not thinking.

RCS: I'm not sure I understand you now.

HEIDEGGER: Thinking is, ultimately, thinking about one thing only, Being. Anything else is mere curiosity. And talking about anything else is merely idle chatter.

RCS: What about our conversation now? Are we thinking? Am I gaining *understanding* from you?

HEIDEGGER: That depends on you, of course, and how resolute you are about understanding. How serious you are. And it has nothing to do with me; I am merely a spokesman. Being thinks *through* me. Perhaps, someday, through you, too.

RCS: That sounds like Hegel, and the idea of universal spirit picking him as its spokesman. Do you see yourself as part of that tradition?

HEIDEGGER: I reject the tradition. But yes, I do find essential affinities with Hegel, in particular, as well as with his younger friend Schelling. They too were *thinkers*.

RCS: But let me be sure I understand what we've said so far; you see the essence of becoming ourselves, or the essence of being a *Dasein,* in terms of understanding *Being* . . .

HEIDEGGER: Which means, first, understanding oneself, the being through whom Being comes into question.

RCS: And understanding mainly means feeling "at home" in the world, not knowledge in the traditional sense. But that feeling can come only through the great effort of what you call *thinking,* which means breaking away from the undifferentiated everydayness of being *das Man* and facing one's own death resolutely and thinking about Being, including the being that one is as *Dasein,* but not necessarily doing anything in particular. [*catches breath and takes a large gulp of beer.*]

HEIDEGGER: That is very much oversimplified, indeed rather simpleminded. But perhaps it is a beginning.

RCS: Thank you.

HEIDEGGER: But we have said nothing yet about care (*Sorge*). Perhaps that will help you to understand why I have rebelled against the tradition.

RCS: Please proceed!

HEIDEGGER: Philosophers have spoken so often about knowledge and contemplation and consciousness and ideas that they have neglected the real nature of *Dasein,* which is care. I define care as "ahead-of-itself-already-being-(in-the-world)-as-being-near-to (beings encountered in the world)."

RCS: You mean, more simply, that people care; they have worries and concerns.

HEIDEGGER: [*irritably*] If I simply meant that, I would have said so.

RCS: So care is, although I know you reject this idea, the basic structure of consciousness.

HEIDEGGER: Care is the fundamental existential structure of *Dasein.*

RCS: And I notice that you define care in terms of time, that is, in temporal terms such as "being ahead of" and "already."

HEIDEGGER: Yes, in fact you might notice that the three parts of my definition of "care" neatly divide into the three components of time—the past, the present and the future. To be *Dasein* is to be temporal; to be *Dasein* is to care; to care is to exist in time.

RCS: But you mean something very special by "time," do you not?

HEIDEGGER: Yes, of course. I do not mean mere "clock time" of the sort that is measured by that watch you are wearing, your badge of rank in our inauthentic technological society. I mean the authentic time that can only be measured *within Dasein,* the sense of the presence and the passing of one's own *existenz.*

RCS: You mean, for example, the fact that, sitting in a philosophy lecture, which in fact lasts exactly fifty minutes, it *seems* to me that it has lasted two-and-one-half hours. Is that what you mean?

HEIDEGGER: The fact that you say "seems to" suggests that you consider the clock time to be true, and your own sense of time to be untrue. Is that not so?

RCS: I guess so; but you would say that one's own sense of time is more true?

HEIDEGGER: More *eigentlich*. More important for our understanding of Being.

RCS: And that means, I suppose, that the ultimate fact about time is the impending fact of one's own death, right?

HEIDEGGER: That is indeed essential, but I would not say "ultimate." Every moment is, in a sense, ultimate, because *Dasein* at every moment decides its own existence, by taking hold of itself or by neglecting itself. And this means thinking about Being through Time.

RCS: I have always thought of Being itself as timeless.

HEIDEGGER: That is because you have been trapped in the tradition. Being *is* time as well as *in* time and *through* time, and both Being and Time come to be issues through *Dasein*.

RCS: But do Being and Time exist apart from us?

HEIDEGGER: You are still caught in the tradition. What do you mean, "apart from us"? as if we were separated from being, and ourselves outside of time.

RCS: I see what you mean.

HEIDEGGER: Perhaps you do not appreciate the clever Teutonic thoroughness with which I have constructed my system. Look, let me explain it to you quite simply: I have said that *Dasein* is essentially the being through whom Being and its own Being come into question. I have also said that *Dasein* is essentially care, and care is in turn defined in terms of time—past, present, and future. Let me show you how all of this ties together.

RCS: Yes, please do.

HEIDEGGER: [*picks a napkin from the table, on which he begins a list*] Dasein has three essential structures, or, more simply, *existentialia*. These are *existenz, facticity* and *falleness*. We have already spoken about *existenz;* it consists of our possibilities, and particularly, the possibility of understanding. Only *Dasein* has possibilities . . .

RCS: Doesn't an acorn have possibilities, that is, the possibility of growing into an oak tree, the possibility of providing a home for squirrels, the possibility of . . .

HEIDEGGER: No. Now *existenz,* you notice, explicitly concerns the future. Possibilities are always in the future. It is *existenz* that requires *Dasein* to decide, to choose itself, to resolve what it is and what it will be.

RCS: And death too, is in the future.

HEIDEGGER: Of course. *Existenz,* in other words, is essentially the possibility of understanding one's own Being, and that means living in the uncertainty of the future.

RCS: And *facticity*? That is a term I know from M. Sartre.

HEIDEGGER: And from where do you think he stole it? Our facticity is our past. It is the fact that we find ourselves in a world that is not of our choosing, born in this house of these parents, at this time in history, and faced with one set of decisions rather than others.

RCS: That is what you sometimes call "being thrown in the world."

HEIDEGGER: Yes, *Geworfenheit.* We come to appreciate facticity, however, not so much in reflection and thought as in our day-to-day moods (*Stimme*) or what I call by the profound expression "being tuned" (*Gestimmtsein*) into the world. It is in moods that our facticity is disclosed to us. But it is also in one mood, in particular, *angst,* that our *existenz* is disclosed to us, as well.

RCS: Sounds quite gloomy. What about hope?

HEIDEGGER: [*ignores the question and raises his voice*] And then there is the third existential structure, which I call *Fallenness.* Fallenness is allowing oneself to remain a captive of the everyday, forgetting one's *existenz* and literally "falling" back into undifferentiated everydayness.

RCS: We spoke about this earlier. I take it that one can fall only after he has risen, that is, has begun to understand and think about Being. So the difference between undifferentiated everydayness and fallenness is that one falls only *after* one has begun to understand. And that is the nature of inauthenticity, too; it is "falling" once one has already begun to understand what it is to be authentic.

HEIDEGGER: Yes, authenticity and inauthenticity are two modes of existence for *Dasein,* whereas *existenz,* facticity and fallenness are existential structures. These three structures are present in every *Dasein,* but the two modes are more ideals, in that no one could ever be perfectly authentic, nor could anyone ever fall into total inauthenticity.

RCS: Does that mean that you yourself aren't authentic, Professor?

HEIDEGGER: I have come to reconsider these modes of existence by reconsidering the question of Being.

RCS: But wait; before we go on, it seems that you are listing a series of parallel threes, past, present and future; *existenz,* facticity, and fallenness . . .

HEIDEGGER: No, *existenz* goes with the future, facticity with the past, and fallenness with the present.

RCS: Sorry; I didn't mention them in order.

HEIDEGGER: And then there are three aspects of being-in-the-world: discovery of oneself as already in the world (*befindlichkeit*) or the recognition and interpretation of one's facticity; understanding (*verstehen*) of course, which is the realization of one's *existenz*; and there is discourse (*rede*) which is the capacity to articulate our being "tuned in" to the world and what Understanding discloses to us.

RCS: You mean understanding is prior to articulation?

HEIDEGGER: It is speech that discloses to us the nature of Being. Language is the house of Being.

RCS: [*pauses, puzzled*] Does that mean that authenticity is merely being able to speak? Or is discourse the mark of fallenness?

HEIDEGGER: No, no, no! I did not say that the three modes of comportment were exactly correlated with the three existential structures. One can "fall" through language, but only through the mode of inauthenticity.

RCS: So what you have just mentioned are three characteristics of authenticity. To be authentic is to recognize both facticity and *existenz,* and to articulate them through speech.

HEIDEGGER: Yes, their inauthentic counterparts would be *ambiguity,* in which *Dasein* finds himself caught up in a whirlpool of endless chores and activities . . .

RCS: So everyday activity is not itself inauthentic; that condition exists when one is totally "caught up" in everydayness, without any further perspective.

HEIDEGGER: And in inauthenticity, one dispenses with the hard thinking of Understanding and settles for mere *curiosity.* One might be quite clever in this, even devoting one's life to it, as a research scientist or an analyst of one sort or another, but that is not understanding, it is not authentic. Inauthenticity makes it impossible for us to choose ourselves.

RCS: Why is that?

HEIDEGGER: Because it neglects Being; because it is forget-fulness. Because it is *self*-forgetting.

RCS: And what would the third characterization be?

HEIDEGGER: What I call "prattle" (*gerede*), mere idle *chatter.* Political conversations, most philosophy, and discussions about the best restaurant in town are all idle chatter. They have nothing to do with Being.

RCS: May I get you another beer?

HEIDEGGER: [*ignores the query*] In fact, idle chatter defines our whole modern existence. No one knows how to think anymore. Even our language has lost its ability to allow us to think.

RCS: This is why you think poetry is superior to philosophy?

HEIDEGGER: Poetry *is* philosophy. It is language refinding itself.

RCS: Is that why you, in effect, have been making up your own language?

HEIDEGGER: Yes, of course. You Americans think I am being perverse, but it is language that is perverse, your own in par-ticular. It is only German, and also ancient Greek, that allows for thinking.

RCS: That is why you talk about only German and Greek phil-osophers?

HEIDEGGER: Yes; conveniently, those are the languages I read best—and Latin, of course. But the point is this—that the very structure of language is such that it makes us misunderstand. For example, a sentence is in the form of a subject, then a predicate, "I see the X," and so we think automatically of a subject that sees, and an X that is seen.

RCS: That sounds very much like Nietzsche's lament "I am afraid we have to believe in God because we still believe in gram-mar."

HEIDEGGER: Yes, like Hegel too. But what you must appreciate is the fact that I work very hard at my language constructions, and what I am trying to do is extremely difficult—to reconstruct language so that it more accurately reflects the nature of Being. I am not perversely obscure . . .

RCS: I have heard that you would revise sentences in your seminars if anyone understood them.

HEIDEGGER: *Mis*understood them. In every case, it is Being that I am trying to express; having others understand me is a secondary concern.

RCS: Oh.

HEIDEGGER: Public language is inadequate; I must invent my own.

RCS: But you are still using German. A particular language. If "language is the house of Being" as you say, aren't you worried that Being might live in several very different houses? And be different for every language?

HEIDEGGER: Frankly, that has begun to worry me.

RCS: Do you think *any* language can be constructed to express adequately what you call "Being"?

HEIDEGGER: I am no longer so certain.

RCS: How do you know that the language you are inventing won't become a mere personal expression, or even a private language that no one else, perhaps not even you, will be able to understand?

HEIDEGGER: I think we have pursued this very interesting line of questioning far enough. I think that I must go very soon, as it is a considerable drive for me to get back home.

RCS: Average everydayness strikes again.

HEIDEGGER: Eh?

RCS: Oh, nothing. [*pauses*] By the way, we have not spoken of Nothing.

HEIDEGGER: And there is much about Nothing of which to speak.

RCS: May we speak about Nothing?

HEIDEGGER: Nothing doing!

RCS: You mean, "nothing nothings."

HEIDEGGER: Yes, that is what Nothing does.

RCS: Aren't we talking nonsense?

HEIDEGGER: No. We are talking metaphysics.

RCS: What about nothing?

HEIDEGGER: He who speaks of nothing does not know what he is doing; to speak of nothing is illogical.

RCS: But you are an irrationalist, aren't you?

HEIDEGGER: Irrationalism is only the obvious weakness of rationalism, and therefore itself a kind of rationalism.

RCS: But does it make sense to speak of nothing?

HEIDEGGER: So you want nothing to "make sense"; that is not where truth is to be found.

RCS: Is the truth to be found in nothingness?

HEIDEGGER: To speak of nothing will always remain a horror and an absurdity for common sense, but, yes, the truth is to be found in Nothing, for Nothing is Being, as well, so long as it is not confused with Something.

RCS: You mean the possibility of nonexistence, the contingency of all things and everything, is an essential part of our living with them?

HEIDEGGER: Yes, but Nothing is not just the other side of Being; it is at one with what-is-in-totality.

RCS: You have said that it is dread that reveals Nothing to us; are you speaking again of our sense of our own impending death?

HEIDEGGER: "Death" is not a term that is adequate to Being, and therefore it is not adequate to Nothing, either.

RCS: Wait! The one thing I thought I did understand was our selves as *Dasein* as Being-unto-Death.

HEIDEGGER: That is much too simpleminded and not what I meant at all.

RCS: But you said that Dread is a mood through which we apprehend Nothing . . .

HEIDEGGER: Dread is not an apprehension of Nothing, but all the same, Nothing is revealed in and through Dread. In Dread, what-is-in-totality becomes untenable.

RCS: So in the end there is Nothing?

HEIDEGGER: In the end is Being. Or rather, standing within the disclosure of Being is what I call the *existenz* of man.

RCS: So man is Being?

HEIDEGGER: No, Man is only the mask of Being.

RCS: Then we know only the appearance of Being?

HEIDEGGER: No. No! NO! You obviously have not understood anything I have been telling you all night. It has been a wasted evening.

RCS: I'm sorry, Professor, but could you just tell me . . .

HEIDEGGER: No! No! No! I'm going home. Being is the mission of thought, and the thinker utters Being. Language uses man and so discloses Being to Itself. I can see that you have understood nothing at all. Nothing at all! A wasted evening! A wasted evening!

RCS: May I give you a ride, Professor?

HEIDEGGER: A wasted evening. A wasted evening. No, I do not want a ride. Thought is the devotion to Being, and nothing else. You have understood nothing, thought about nothing, especially not Nothing. Good night. Good night.

RCS: [*glumly*] Good night, Professor.

"Let's not beat around the bush; I love life—that's my real weakness. I love it so much I am incapable of imagining what is not life."

—from *The Fall*

3   *Albert Camus*

I first read Camus in the early 1950s while I was in high school. In fact, his may have been the only book I read in high school. One of my better-read friends (a type who would come to be called "beatnik") encouraged me to read her copy of *The Stranger*. The book had been published almost ten years before, and it had become an instant best–seller in Paris, skyrocketing its young Algerian author to a fame for which he was not yet prepared and had difficulty surviving. It wasn't until 1946, however, that this work was translated into English, after which it began to filter down to the cultural proletariat of American youth, along with the word "existentialism." None of us knew what the expression meant—or rather, it seemed to mean anything anyone cared for it to mean. It was a word that sounded full of meaning, and *The Stranger* was a book that fit well into our prevailing world of nuclear bomb threats and air raid drills, James Dean, the beginning of network television, and rigid high school dress codes. (Long hair or blue jeans and you were out!) Meursault, the "stranger" in Camus' text was indeed a hero to us. (We didn't know then what an 'anti-hero' is.) Innocent and admirable in his simplicity, Meursault knew how to enjoy the sun, how not to worry, how to *live*. He felt no guilt, regretted nothing, entertained no phony emotions, no pretentions, no ambitions. And even when he found himself in what would seem the most terrifying of situations—accused of a senseless murder and condemned to death by a travesty of a trial—he remained unperturbed, uninvolved, still "happy." We didn't know what to make of it, but we knew that something important had been shown to us. The book changed our perspectives, if not our lives. (High school doesn't lend itself to existential revolt.) But we wanted to be so mindless, so innocent, so happy, ourselves. On the other hand, as Camus had his characters say, nothing in our lives ever really changes anyway.

It was with a special sense of anticipation, therefore, that in 1957 I waited for M. Camus in Stockholm, where the next day he was to receive the Nobel Prize for literature. Unlike his former friend (recently turned enemy) Jean-Paul Sartre, who would turn down the prize seven years later, Camus would graciously accept the esteemed award. It was mid-October, and Stockholm was predictably foul—damp, chilly, grey, gloomy. As I bundled myself against the cold, a dramatic contrast came into my mind's eye:

cold, austere Scandinavia juxtaposed to the hot sun of Camus' novels, beating down on the sea, beaches, and desert of northwest Africa.

Like Plato and so many other northern European authors, Camus used the sun to represent life, truth, and happiness—a deadly force but one transcending death as well. I pictured Camus basking on the beach in Algeria like his character Meursault, the sun burning away his cares, leaving a vacuum that he himself would no doubt call "happiness." In 1957, of course, it had been many years since he had been in his homeland, which had been ravaged by a brutal civil war punctuated by daily acts of terrorism on both sides—a tragedy which troubled him deeply.

He appeared a few minutes late—not fashionably late but as if he had been delayed by a great distraction with which he was faced. His handsome face bore a rugged, frowning look almost too serious not to be mistaken as a pose. Immediately, I thought of Humphrey Bogart—a resemblance that came to mind repeatedly. Camus wore a dark tan trenchcoat, tied tight around the middle—a Bogie trademark—with the collar thrown back around his head, as much like a halo as protection against the drizzle. Brow still furrowed, he gave me a boyish smile and extended his hand—the one without the hand-rolled cigarette, one of a continuous chain. He had the kind of charm that made me like him immediately, for no reason whatever. I restrained myself, of course, stood up stiffly, awkwardly, grabbed his hand, and we both sat down.

I then remembered this scene, two strangers meeting in a café, sheltered from a persistent drizzle outside, as the setting of Camus' latest novel, *The Fall*. His readers in Paris had been shocked by the cynical pessimism of its tone—so unlike his earlier works. Its story—that of a brilliantly successful lawyer who had "dropped out," turning against himself and all of society—projected a relentlessly dark view of modern morals. Not surprisingly, many critics took that voice to be Camus' own, now drastically changed from the happy naiveté of *The Stranger,* written fifteen years earlier. Set in a seedy bar in the gloomy inner canals of Amsterdam, *The Fall* was also an interview of sorts, with Camus' appropriately gloomy character Clamence wholly dominating the conversation, turning himself as a mirror to his speechless companion, to make him judge and condemn himself. I wondered if that would be the course of our own discussion—if the Camus who had defended the joy of living and that innocent independence of *The Stranger* had indeed become the bitter "judge-penitent" of *The Fall*. I worried that I too was about to be put on trial. But such fears were quickly put to rest. M. Camus was almost too polite, like a schoolboy applying for a position; and whereas he would give thoughtful, almost painful answers to whatever I would ask, it was evident that he was not going to *take* me anywhere. Like Meursault, he was resigned to drift with an indifferent contentment wherever we happened to go. I quickly learned that the category that best fit Camus, as well as his philosophy—in direct contrast to the philosophy of Sartre—was that of resignation. Like his allegorical hero, Sisyphus, who was forever condemned to pushing a rock up a hill only to have it fall back again, Camus resigned himself to his fate, his revolt against the absurdity of life confined to a passive if also aggressive refusal to add to its cruelty. I could see how easily he would infuriate the Leftist revolutionaries.

Because I had interviewed few philosophers, I was at a loss to know how to start. "What is the absurd?" Uh, uh . . . too much like an exam question, I decided. "What do you think of the recent philosophy of M. Sartre?" No, my readers want to meet Camus, not hear what (overly polite) defenses he would muster against his more brilliant antagonist. I thought to ask, "And how is Missus Sisyphus?"—a kind of alliterative joke which had occurred to me on the train to Sweden, and also a swipe at Camus' consciously male-dominated philosophy. But that surely would not get things off to a very promising start. So, as a beginning, I decided to do what I often do on a first date—so to speak—and that was to comment about the weather:

RCS: You must hate all this rain.

CAMUS: [*politely, indifferently*] I don't really mind it.

RCS: You must miss Algeria.

CAMUS: I always feel a little in exile, if that's what you mean. But my life is here—in Paris, that is. In Stockholm, I just feel like another wet tourist.

RCS: What do you remember most about Algeria?

CAMUS: If you mean now, I think of my homeland with a kind of despair, although that is an emotion which I have always despised. What can you do when your friends are intent on destroying themselves in the name of absolute "principles"?

RCS: I actually meant the Algeria you remember from twenty years ago, or even before that, as a child.

CAMUS: The two really can't be separated; innocence and regret are complements, like love and despair. It is the loss of the first that breeds the second. And to me Algeria still represents a kind of innocence, I would even say "truth." Algeria is stark, simple;

the sun clarifies everything. There are no shadows. Life and death coexist with a dreadful cooperation—the fertile fields next to the parched desert, Roman ruins in bustling, overcrowded cities. Resignation goes hand in hand with revolt—just the opposite of Paris, which believes in neither. A stoic calm is punctuated by eruptions of sudden and passionate violence. There has always been sudden violence, you see, but now it is different, wholly rational, political, meaningless. It used to be that when a man believed his girl friend had betrayed him, he killed her. Now, they go to a café and both are blown to bits by terrorists.

RCS: Let's talk about the violence in *The Stranger*. Meursault shoots an Arab, in self-defense perhaps, but seemingly, from his own description, for no reason at all. Let me read what has become one of the most celebrated passages in recent literature:

> Then everything began to reel before my eyes, a fiery gust came from the sea, while the sky cracked in two, from end to end, and a great sheet of flame poured down through the rift. Every nerve in my body was a steel spring, and my grip closed on the revolver. The trigger gave, and the smooth underbelly of the butt jogged my palm. And so, with that crisp, whipcrack sound, it all began. I shook off my sweat and the clinging veil of light. I knew I'd shattered the balance of the day, the spacious calm of this beach on which I had been happy. But I fired four shots more into the inert body, on which they left no visible trace. And each successive shot was another loud, fateful rap on the door of my undoing. [p. 76]

CAMUS: But notice that nowhere in that passage does Meursault see himself as actually *doing* anything: "the trigger gave," "the smooth underbelly of the butt jogged my palm." He is as much a victim of the Newtonian reaction of the revolver as the Arab is the victim of the bullet. And as for what you call "reasons," couldn't the heat of the sun be just as much a "reason" as what you call "self-defense"? In Meursault's mind, the one makes as much sense as the other. In fact, the real violence is the heat of the sun—perhaps you might even say that the sun is the murderer, for it is only the sun that is the active force in this scene.

RCS: I agree that there is indeed something peculiarly passive about that scene, but I do not view it so much in the context of what "makes sense" as in the context of what significance *you* give to it in the novel. Why, for example, is self-defense never raised as an issue at Meursault's trial? How incompetent could his lawyer be, not to even mention it? Why does he let the prosecutor get away with, in effect, condemning him to death for not visibly grieving for his mother?

CAMUS: But the point of the trial, of course, is not to make a display of Algerian justice, but to create a vehicle for Meursault's loss of innocence. You see, that loss is not through his crime but after it, when he is forced to see himself through the eyes of others, to judge himself as a criminal, a murderer, as guilty.

RCS: But the trial itself is surely a farce. Meursault watches the flies while he is sentenced to death. That doesn't seem much like a serious philosophical vehicle.

CAMUS: But it is, of course, and that's just the point. There is a sense in which my admittedly overdrawn prosecutor is correct when he says that he "looked inside of the murderer's soul, and found not a trace of those moral qualities, the least spark of human feeling." Meursault's innocence is indeed inhuman, and explicitly devoid of—or prior to—morality. Given the senselessness of the crime and Meursault's total sense of detachment from it, it makes little difference whether he is accused of this crime or some other. So the prosecutor's bizarre accusation, that Meursault is just as guilty of the next crime on the dock—a parricide—is not wholly pointless.

RCS: Conor Cruise O'Brien has written what I would consider to be a definitive objection to your trial, whatever its philosophical purpose. He rightly insists that a French court in Algeria would never condemn a European to death for shooting an Arab, especially an Arab who had drawn a knife on him and who had already stabbed another European. Imagine a murder trial in the American South—in a Faulkner novel, perhaps—in which a white man is hanged for killing a black man who had attacked him. That is wholly implausible, isn't it? And O'Brien rightly concludes, and I think I agree, that this sense of unreality on your part betrays your own colonial insensitivity.

CAMUS: Nonsense. The novel is not "about" colonialism in Africa, but "about" Meursault and his passage from innocence to reflection. The trial is a vehicle and so is the murder itself.

RCS: But isn't it true that the whole novel indicates the same sense of unreality regarding the Arabs? The Arabs, unlike the Europeans, are never given names. The Arab that Meursault kills is not even described. All we see is Meursault's own discomfort.

CAMUS: It is true that the Arabs are "unreal" to Meursault, mere figures, not people with whom he communicates. Perhaps your good humanists in northern Europe may bemoan from their impersonal distance that lack of mutual understanding which is so obvious to anyone who has lived with it all his life, but the fact is that such is the case. The Arabs *are* different, they are in their own world, which excludes ours. And Meursault's way of seeing them, even if he is "strange" and peculiarly unreflective, is not all that different from the colonial view as such.

RCS: Isn't that in itself an indictment of colonialism?

CAMUS: Cultural differences are real enough, unavoidable and unregrettable. The problem in Algeria, as I have argued for nearly twenty years, is a *political* problem, not a cultural one, but that surely has nothing to do with *The Stranger.* The novel does not "indict" anyone or anything. It does not take a stand, except perhaps for life. If I wrote a poem about springtime, I'm sure some of your friends would say that I am, by neglect of the "real" issues, furthering the cause of capitalism and imperialism. I wish they were less engaged in "the issues" and more engaged in their lives. Anyway, no, my novel is not even implicitly an indictment of colonialism, nor need I apologize for my own ambiguities. Algeria, after all, was—perhaps still is—my home. I cannot view it through the single lens of some abstract ideology.

RCS: You did say, if forced to choose between your mother and justice, you would choose your mother?

CAMUS: Yes, I did, although it's often been quoted out of context. Justice is an honorable abstraction, but still an abstraction, perhaps impossible to realize. Politics has become nothing but abstractions, devoid of those simple personal feelings of one human being for another . . .

RCS: Such as a son's love for his mother?

CAMUS: Precisely. Those personal, human affections are the only legitimate motive for justice, and when they come into conflict— the abstract ideal and the feelings—there is only one way I can choose.

RCS: If we may return to *The Stranger:* the image of the mother, who we learn in the first sentence is dead ("Mother died today, or was it yesterday''), haunts the book even to the extent of becoming the dominant figure of Meursault's trial, the reason for his death, as well as his philosophical mentor as he awaits his execution.

CAMUS: That image too is a device, of course. Especially in

France—but not only in France—a son's attachment to his mother, and his sense of loss at her death, must be among the most basic of all feelings, even for the most wicked person among us. The fact that Meursault does not feel even this indicates the extreme simplicity and—should I say—the vacuity of his feelings. If he can't feel this, he must have no emotions at all. And I would say again that it is in this sense that he is wholly innocent.

RCS: You keep referring to Meursault's "innocence," but surely his total indifference is much more than that?

CAMUS: It is not "total indifference." He loves the sun and the smells of the sea. He shows a sensitivity to his own sensations that we can only dimly imagine. He even bends continually to the feelings of others, commenting each time, "if it would please them." But yes, he is strikingly indifferent to most emotions— particularly regret—as well as guilt, envy, and hatred. It is this that makes him "strange."

RCS: Indifferent also to love?

CAMUS: Yes, love too. When Marie asks him if he loves her, Meursault responds by commenting that her question has no meaning, and tells us "I supposed that I didn't."

RCS: Sounds sadistic to me, either stupid or cruel.

CAMUS: Murder may also be stupid or cruel, but in Meursault's simple vision, it is all the same.

RCS: But why call that "innocence"?

CAMUS: In order to insist that so many of our feelings are manufactured, artificial, such as lies we tell ourselves and others about what we *ought* to feel. What is the reason for regret? Or guilt? Or jealousy? When Marie has other plans, Meursault is only "curious." Wouldn't we too be happier if we were simply curious, instead of defensive, frustrated, fearful? And even of love, I have written (in *Myth of Sisyphus*) that "I know only that mixture of desire, affection and intelligence that binds me to this or that creature. . . . I have no right to call these different experiences by the same name." What we call love, with its commitments and unreal promises, is a fabrication, an illusion, not really an emotion at all.

RCS: I would say that you do not know what an emotion is. You confuse the intelligence of emotions with what you call their artificiality. Most emotions, including all those you've mentioned, are complex responses to the world which Meursault in his simplicity cannot grasp. That does not make him more honest, or we less so. It makes him inhuman. He will not reflect or judge, and because emotions require such reflection and judgments, he cannot feel, except for the simplest sensations.

CAMUS: Do you deny the attraction of that simplicity?

RCS: No, I felt it myself when I first read the book, as an adolescent. But now I would say that Meursault "secretes the inhuman," as you've said elsewhere, that he does not have the least sense of those human qualities that the Greeks called "rationality," including emotions.

CAMUS: You now sound like my prosecutor.

RCS: I know I do, but I object to Meursault not as a character but as a hero, even an "absurd hero," if you like. For example, a few years ago you wrote, if I may read it to you [*opens book and begins reading*], that

> . . . the hero of the book is condemned because he doesn't play the game. In this sense he is a stranger to the society in which he lives; he drifts in the margin, in the suburb of private, solitary, sensual life. This is why some readers are tempted to consider him as a waif. You will have a more precise idea of this character, or one at all events in closer conformity with the intentions of the author, if you ask yourself in what way Meursault doesn't play the game. The answer is simple: He refuses to lie. Lying is not only saying what is not true. It is also and especially saying more than is true and, as far as the human heart is concerned, saying more than one feels. This is what we all do every day to simplify life. Meursault, despite appearances, does not wish to simplify life. He says what is true. He refuses to disguise his feelings and immediately society feels threatened. He is asked, for example, to say that he regrets his crime according to the ritual formula. He replies that he feels about it more annoyance than real regret and this shade of meaning condemns him.
>
> Meursault for me is then not a waif, but a man who is poor and naked, in love with the sun which leaves no shadows. Far from it being true that he lacks all sensibility, a deep tenacious passion animates him, a passion for the absolute and for truth. It is a still negative truth, the truth of being and of feeling, but one without which no victory over oneself and over the world will ever be possible.
>
> You would not be far wrong then in reading *The Stranger* as a story of a man who, without any heroics,

accepts death for the sake of truth. I have sometimes said, and always paradoxically, that I have tried to portray in this character the only Christ we deserved. You will understand after these explanations that I said this without any intention of blasphemy and only with the slightly ironic affection which an artist has the right to feel towards the characters whom he has created.

CAMUS: You will allow me to indulge in my characters, of course. But what you are describing is indeed what Meursault learns at his trial, how to reflect, how to judge, and how to feel.

RCS: Could you look at Meursault in Part I as an example of what Heidegger calls "average everydayness," a man who goes through life in a purely routine way, taking things as they come and doing things as they are to be done, until facing death in Part II forces him to reflect on what he is and what he has done?

CAMUS: Yes, I would agree that Meursault fits Heidegger's philosophy rather well. It is important that, once he has learned to reflect, he reflects on his simple life and wholly approves it and that he suffers no regrets. He says, "I'd been right, I was still right, I was always right. I passed my life in a certain way; I might have passed it in a different way. I hadn't done x whereas I'd done y or z." It is that sense—that reflective sense—Meursault's rebellion against the regret and despair he is supposed to feel—that makes him an "absurd hero," a hero in the face of the Absurd.

RCS: Which brings us finally to the main point of your whole philosophy, the famous "Absurd." For haven't you written that the absurd is just this love of life in the face of meaninglessness?

CAMUS: No, the absurd is the lack of meaning, not the love of life, which I thoroughly admire. I do not believe in transcendent meanings, meanings beyond our experience. If there is a God but I can't know Him, for example, what difference is it to me whether He exists or not?

RCS: That is what you mean when you write, "It is necessary to live without appeal"?

CAMUS: Yes, but let me be sure that you have understood me. I do not mean and have never said that life is itself absurd or meaningless. And above all I do not believe that life is not worth living. Indeed, that is the whole point of *Myth of Sisyphus,* and I am bewildered by those who take it to be a demonstration of the opposite. And it is not just God that offers us the illusion of a transcendent meaning, but any view that sacrifices the present to ent to the future—marxism, for instance—or to the past—some people's obsession with history, for example.

RCS: Would you say that the absurd is the central theme of your philosophy?

CAMUS: Well, it once may have been, although now I am far more concerned with the cruelty of men to each other than I am about what in the forties I called "the indifference of the universe." But even then, if you reread *The Stranger* or *The Myth,* you will find that the dominant single concept is not absurdity but happiness, although the two themes are often found together.

RCS: Explain that.

CAMUS: I believe that love of life is the highest virtue. And life is absurd—in the sense that we cannot comprehend it, find its purpose, its meaning. And so we revolt against that absurdity, create meanings in the face of the Absurd, not denying it but confronting it, keeping it alive. To use up everything that we are given, to assert our will to live without hope or meaning—that is happiness.

RCS: Like Sisyphus, in other words, who you insist is happy because he defies the gods and the hopelessness of his tasks.

CAMUS: Yes, not just to live without appeal but, first and foremost, to live.

RCS: I'm never quite certain I understand what "the Absurd" amounts to. The common idea seems to be that life is absurd because absurd things happen, events without meaning. That doesn't seem to be the point of the Sisyphus myth, however.

CAMUS: Whatever "meaning" an event may possess is a matter of what we do with it. The meaning of Meursault's actions was wholly outside of him, a matter of interpretation in which he himself would not indulge . . .

RCS: Could not indulge?

CAMUS: Whatever. But absurd events do not constitute the Absurd. The Absurd is the stupid density of the world, a density we attempt to illuminate with metaphors and illusions. A world understood with bad reasons is still familiar to us. A world explained by appeal, to God or justice or capitalism, for example, is a world in which one can resign oneself to apparent absurdity, denying the Absurd. It is against such hopes and resignation that I insist on revolting.

RCS: I still don't quite understand. Leaving aside the revolt for a moment, what is it that you are revolting against? If the Absurd does not consist of absurdities, what is it?

CAMUS: It is first of all a kind of experience, a sensibility. Sartre has a beautiful example in his novel, *Nausea,* in which his hero looks in horror at the root of a tree and is overwhelmed with the sheer presence of it. It is no longer familiar, just *there.* No longer meaningful as a tree root, just this *thing* that confronts him. Sometimes a familiar face, viewed in a certain light, becomes something unfamiliar, horrible. You look at the woman you've lived with for a year, and you realize that you will never understand her, know her—but she is there. It is living in the face of that face that concerns me. But the face is the world itself.

RCS: And so you say that the Absurd is rational man looking for understanding in a universe which will not give it to him.

CAMUS: That's the basic idea.

RCS: Would it be fair to say, as Meursault argues in *The Stranger,* that the Absurd is the inevitable fact of death?

CAMUS: No, because life would be equally absurd for an immortal. Sisyphus, for example, is immortal, and the fact that he does not fear death does not make his life any less absurd; in fact, it makes it even more absurd.

RCS: Is the Absurd then the mere repetition and meaninglessness of his task? Simone de Beauvoir writes of a person who commits suicide out of despair at the senselessness of brushing one's teeth every day.

CAMUS: No, it is not the repetition as such. If I watch a cockroach pushing a crumb up a hill, only to have it fall back again, even forever, that is not the Absurd, at least, not for the cockroach. It is Sisyphus's *consciousness* of the repetition, the utter meaninglessness of his task, that makes him an absurd hero.

RCS: Then how is Meursault also an absurd hero?

CAMUS: It is true that he lacks that essential dimension of consciousness, at least, until the very end of the book. But when he attains it, to confirm his life, he is, in effect, already dead. He lives without hope, it is true, but he also has no hope to live.

RCS: He hopes that there will be hope, however. He toys with the idea of giving condemned men a chance, even one chance in a million, just a ray of hope, if only it weren't so certain.

CAMUS: Yes. But he does not get that chance, and in that subtle point lies the whole secret of the condemned man, who is indifferent to every detail of life and so intensely aware of nothing but the flame of life itself.

RCS: You say that Sisyphus is absurd because he is conscious of his absurdity; Meursault is not absurd because he is not conscious. Is the Absurd a philosophical viewpoint, then—a way of thinking—or is it, as you sometimes say, a "sensibility"?

CAMUS: It is both, of course. There are things that the heart can feel which we may not yet articulate, and the Absurd is one of them. That is why I often talk about it as a "revolt of the flesh." The body knows its limitations; the philosophical mind sometimes does not.

RCS: Is that why you give so little attention to the philosophers, even those whom you quote and discuss? For example, you say, "At any street-corner the Absurd can hit a man in the face" and, in one of your most powerful examples, you describe an average working day:

> Rising, streetcar, four hours in the office or factory, meal, streetcar, four hours of work, meal, sleep, and Monday Tuesday Wednesday Thursday Friday and Saturday according to the same rhythm. . . . But one day the "why?" arises and everything begins in that weariness tinged with amazement.

CAMUS: I think it is essential that the experience I am describing is a "common" experience, that is, not merely the construction of a few philosophers, in which case I would not even think about it.

RCS: Is Sisyphus really the model for all of us, then? Surely, our lives are not so brazenly joyless. We do not have to face the prospect of immortality. And we are not alone, at least, on our mountain.

CAMUS: Neither is Sisyphus, actually. He has the gods watching over him, the gods whom he dares to defy.

RCS: Well, that is another difference, isn't it? And a crucial one for your philosophy. We do not have a god to scorn, which is what you claim is the very essence of the Absurd.

CAMUS: True, but that doesn't mean that we can't scorn the *absence* of God—for ultimately, irrational gods or the nonexistence of a rational God amount to the same. In both cases, our complaints avail us nothing. They are mere gestures.

RCS: That reminds me of your example of a man talking in a phone booth: we see his violent gestures but we don't hear the conversation. You say that he is absurd. "We wonder why he is alive," you say.

CAMUS: Yes, it is that sense of communication that is missing.

RCS: But, of course, someone is on the other end, giving his gestures their meaning.

CAMUS: But suppose there were not? Just suppose the man were there, shouting and gesticulating wildly to nothing and no one. Perhaps that is what we are like—and Sisyphus too.

RCS: But you say Sisyphus has a "silent joy." You say "one must imagine Sisyphus happy." Why?

CAMUS: Because he lives. His revolt is his scornful acceptance of his task. It is his struggle toward the heights that fulfills him— not just pushing the rock up the mountain, of course, but his sense of defiance in making his meaningless task meaningful.

RCS: Sounds like resentment to me.

CAMUS: Can you draw the line between revolt and resentment?

RCS: How about impotence?

CAMUS: But Sisyphus isn't impotent at all. He cannot throw away his rock, of course, but his fate belongs to him, and no one or nothing else.

RCS: It stills sounds impotent as a "revolt" —I would even say "reactionary."

CAMUS: It is a "reaction" —against the absurd.

RCS: But a gesture or a look of contempt is surely not a "revolt."

CAMUS: It can be—especially against the gods. But a more serious answer is this: sometimes *not* the act, or just to live as you are living, is a more profound revolt against human misery than to participate in an active revolution. For example, one can refuse to be a terrorist or an executioner.

RCS: Perhaps that is not particularly relevant to Sisyphus, however.

CAMUS: True, but the point is this: in simple, even passive defiance, in accepting one's life and loving it, under whatever conditions, is the one sense of happiness that is available to us.

RCS: How can philosophy change our lives? You don't seem to tell us to *do* anything; neither does Heidegger. I'm not sure I see the point of it.

CAMUS: One can change a life without *doing* anything differently. That is why one of the most popular devices in French
literature, from Stendhal to Sartre, is the paradox of the man
who realizes his freedom in prison. Meursault is like this, of
course. He cannot *do* anything. He is trapped, helpless. But it is
at that moment one realizes it is how one comes to *see* his situation that means everything—whether he sees himself as a martyr,
a victim, a hero, a scoundrel or whatever.

RCS: That would include Meursault as well?

CAMUS: Of course. His continuing happiness—not the absurd—
is the theme of the novel.

RCS: Happiness is, you have said, the continuous theme in your
work, although your characters don't seem particularly happy,
nor are they ever in happy circumstances. In fact, you have your
Caligula say, "Men die, and they are not happy."

CAMUS: That seems to sum it up. But the linkage between happiness and death is more subtle than that.

RCS: Didn't you once write a novel called *A Happy Death*?

CAMUS: Yes, long ago, before *The Stranger*. In fact, the
character there (called "Mersault") was something of a pro-
totype for Meursault in *The Stranger*.

RCS: Any significance to the fact that you added a "u"?

CAMUS: [*smiles slightly*] No, but Mersault and Meursault were
caught up by *le mort* (death), as we all are, and found a happiness there. *The Stranger,* after all, is a novel about a man who
is innocent, who does not recognize death—even with death all
around him.

RCS: I've never understood Meursault's happiness before his execution. Why should a condemned man suddenly become happy?

CAMUS: Ah, Monsieur, you haven't read your assignment with
sufficient care: Meursault says "I realize I was happy, that I had
always been happy and that I was happy still." So, you see, there
was no "sudden happiness" at all. And I do not say that death
itself is happy—quite the contrary—but I do believe in the divine
availability of the condemned man, with his unbelievable
noninterest in everything except the pure flame of life.

RCS: O.K. But what of your novel *The Plague*? There, too, you
end with "to die a happy death." What makes death happy?

CAMUS: To have lived well, and thoroughly. Living without hope
is not the same as living in despair, as many people think. In
Myth of Sisyphus I once said that a reason worth dying for is also

a reason worth living for. I would say that now too, that death gives reason for life.

RCS: That does sound like Heidegger, who once influenced you—death as "the end" of life.

CAMUS: Ah, yes. But your little pun on "end" is of every significance: death ends life. Of course I agree. But death is not the reason for life—and I didn't say that. It is the fact that we die—that one inexorable fact—that places the weight on life, turns it into everything.

RCS: Sartre once complained that you didn't understand Heidegger.

CAMUS: [*drags on his cigarette, shrugs his shoulders, and presses the butt gently into the ash tray*]

RCS: You don't look forward to dying, I presume? [RCS *smiles, not realizing that in just over two years* Camus *would be dead.*]

CAMUS: [*returns the smile, then frowns*] Of course not. I have too much youth in me for death. But I have this sense of urgency to live. We all do.

RCS: Live in what way?

CAMUS: Just to live. There is no substitute for a moment of life.

RCS: But if I recall, one of your characters—the tyrant Caligula—dies with the realization that he had not lived "correctly," although he certainly lived.

CAMUS: Ah, yes. But that was a remark on freedom—and its abuse. Caligula realized the absurdity of life because he was in a position to have almost any want fulfilled. But he wanted the moon, and he couldn't have it. And he wanted to show men the absurdity of life by making life indeed absurd, by killing men who reason. But he missed the point of the absurd, which is to revolt against it, not to join it. He tried to prove his freedom, but instead he proved his distaste for life.

RCS: Aren't life and freedom the same?

CAMUS: No; although M. Sartre might well agree with you, I do not put so much emphasis on choice as he does, and I do not think it nearly so important as other concerns.

RCS: Such as happiness?

CAMUS: Yes. Meursault, for example, was happy, but it would be beside the point to call him 'free.'

RCS: But he does choose; he tells us that "I chose this life, not that. . . ."

CAMUS: But he also says that it makes no difference.

RCS: What would make a difference?

CAMUS: For Meursault, or for me? [*smiles slightly*]

RCS: For you.

CAMUS: To reduce the amount of suffering in the world, even to save one child.

RCS: So you do take very seriously the importance of responsibility—not very different from Sartre after all.

CAMUS: Yes. But freedom and responsibility are not the same. Sartre is surely free to write his editorials in *Les Temps Modern* about an Algeria he has never seen, a thousand miles away. But responsibility is not that abstraction: it is to live in the middle; "engaged," he would probably say.

RCS: And what would it be, to be "engaged"? How are you, and not he, "engaged," and then responsible for Algeria?

CAMUS: I don't want to be misunderstood. We are both writers, and both far from Oran. The day of the armchair philosopher is over, but neither of us is in there sharing our blood with "the cause."

RCS: The difference is, I presume, that Sartre is willing to have others shed their blood, at least, but you are not.

CAMUS: That is because of a more profound difference: Sartre is sure of what side he is on; I am not.

RCS: Do you mean between the French and the AFC?

CAMUS: Yes. If there were a political party for those who are unsure, that would be my party. I am not one of those who long for the Hungarian people to take up arms again in an uprising doomed to be crushed, under the eyes of an international society which will spare neither applause nor virtuous tears before returning to its slippers, like football enthusiasts on Saturday evening after a big game. There are already too many dead in the stadium, and we can be generous only with our own blood. [*pauses*] But as it is, my party is what Voltaire may have called the party of humanity. As a writer, that is the party I have joined.

RCS: Do you think that a writer can change the world?

CAMUS: No, but I can serve those values that I respect.

RCS: de Beauvoir, Sartre and others have criticized you for not being "a proletarian writer." Do you think that is a legitimate complaint?

CAMUS: Are they "proletarian writers"? There was a famous conversation between Simone de Beauvoir and Simone Weil—our two St. Simone's—and Beauvoir said that the problem of the human condition was the problem of self–identity, to which Weil replied, "then it's obvious that you've never been hungry." So who's the voice of the working class? It's funny, in a way, because I'm the only true working-class writer among them.

RCS: You grew up in rather desperate poverty, from what I've read.

CAMUS: My father died in the First World War. My mother worked as a maid to feed us. That's when I learned about poverty —not from reading Marx, I should say. I grew up in dirty streets, on dirty beaches. Life was hard at home, but the feel of the water washed me clean. I was deeply happy—most of the time.

RCS: Sartre sometimes calls you a "Cartesian of the Absurd." Do you accept that?

CAMUS: [*smiles*] No, too gloomy. But a Cartesian, yes—through and through. I'm French, after all, like Sartre. The duality of consciousness and the physical universe—minus God, of course—is as central to my thinking as to Descartes' three hundred years ago. But I see that duality as a struggle—as does Sartre—not as a divine harmony.

RCS: Why this emphasis on struggle? —which is, I suppose, another way of asking why you think the Absurd is so important.

CAMUS: In my short life, we've been through two world wars, a horrible depression, Algeria, Spain, Auschwitz, world starvation. None of this can be explained away as merely "natural." None of it can be excused by "God's mysterious ways." And yet, we have done it to ourselves. None of us can be innocent any more.

RCS: Are we all guilty then?

CAMUS: No. We are all aware, painfully aware. Our new absurd character (not hero) is (if I may choose one of my own) Clamence, of my latest novel. His absurdity is not what happens to him, but what he does to himself—and then what he does to others.

RCS: What does he do?

CAMUS: He judges them. He deceives. He seduces. He is a hypocrite. None of us can judge others. We have enough to do ourselves. He makes himself unhappy by feeling guilty, and others too. Better than being an ideologue and murdering children, of course, but still, absurd.

RCS: You yourself are not Clamence, then?

CAMUS: No. I read that in the paper, too—that I've gone through "a crisis." No. I am not Clamence. And my next novel will once again be about the sun. [*huddles into his raincoat*]

RCS: If I may be personal—but you've written about it publicly— has your health affected your work?

CAMUS: You mean my tuberculosis—the wages of poverty? When I first became ill as a child and had to drop out of school, I felt betrayed—by what I wasn't sure. I was frightened and bored. I knew I wanted to live. I knew I had to resist. I became deeply aware of life; its dark, ardent flame was deep in my belly. No matter how, or as what, I wanted to live.

RCS: Your disease explains your obsession with death.

CAMUS: No. If anything, it explains my obsession with life.

RCS: Well, it must have seemed "absurd" to you, at the time.

CAMUS: No. I just accepted it as the way things were. As I said, the absurd is a consciousness. I became conscious in that sense only later.

RCS: It must have influenced your novel, *The Plague,* at least.

CAMUS: Well, in an uninteresting sense, yes. But in a more important sense, no. My illness was something I had to go through alone, like Gide's hero in *The Immoralist.* It gave me a sense of my own life as a very intimate existence, *my own.* In *The Plague,* however, the experience is just the opposite: it is the sense of *collective* life, the "engaged" battle, if you like. That sense of individual life is lost, and that is what the novel is about.

RCS: But it is also about evil, and invasion, and the Germans in Paris.

CAMUS: Oh, of course. But surely it is more than an allegory about the German occupation.

RCS: Well, it is about death, the same for us all—you say that too in *The Stranger.*

CAMUS: If you want to say so; but each of us dies—and lives— alone. That much of Heidegger I do understand. And yet, we do it together.

RCS: Sartre complained that *The Plague* is too impersonal, the evil too abstract, the morality too black and white to characterize the very personal and complicated occupation by the Germans.

CAMUS: Yes. That's true. But, as I quote Defoe in the opening page, one prison represents another. *The Plague* may be an impersonal novel but the people who live in it are not depersonalized. It is a heroic novel, a novel about people fighting together, revolting against death. I am not concerned with giving evil a personality.

RCS: The hero of *The Plague,* Dr. Rieux, insists that "heroism doesn't interest me. All that interests me is being a man."

CAMUS: Why do you call Rieux the hero? Because he is a physician? A savior? If *The Plague* has a hero, it is not Rieux but Joseph Grand, who I named so appropriately because he is so *in*significant. He, not Rieux, is a man, and only a man. If Grand is a hero, then, it is because heroism deserves a secondary place. Moreover, what is his heroism? He displays that little bit of human affection. He loves. He works. He loses his love. He regrets. He tries. That's all.

RCS: And he writes.

CAMUS: [*looks up and smiles*] Yes, he writes—poorly. He tries to state his case. He finally deletes all his adjectives.

RCS: I won't ask if you are Grand.

CAMUS: [*another smile*] Thank you.

RCS: Your heroes are so ordinary—Grand, Meursault; are you saying that everyone of us is a hero, then, not only Achilles, Hercules, and the other giants of history and mythology?

CAMUS: Well, not all of my characters are ordinary, Clamence, and Caligula especially; but, yes, I subscribe to that modern notion of heroism according to which we all face death, fight against the absurdities of life, and struggle to survive, if not so dramatically as Hercules. It is life itself that makes us heroes, if we choose to be.

RCS: And your writing? How do you see it now, as you are about to receive the world's most distinguished literary prize?

CAMUS: Surely, it's not so important. But what do you want me to say? There is a Japanese proverb, "A man who rises too quickly in the world makes many enemies." I have mixed feelings. I consider myself a journalist, a stylist, and not, I should say, a philosopher, certainly not a celebrity.

RCS: What of those who have most influenced you? Hemingway, obviously; Gide. Who else?

CAMUS: I don't know why it's important to worry about "influences." The only interesting question seems to me to be, what does a style *do*? Does it capture the truth? If my writing—in *The Stranger,* for example—resembles the American, it is because we share a sense of truth, and the truth is simply stated; it does not need embellished sentences. But I pride myself on my variety of styles. Only *The Stranger,* and some of my essays, is written like that. *The Fall,* on the contrary, is written with utmost attention to an entirely different style, the style of a man who *uses* language, who crucifies himself with its finery and twists the minds of others besides. *The Fall* is filled with subjunctives: you won't find them in the inarticulate mind of Meursault.

RCS: And adjectives?

CAMUS: Yes, *The Fall* is filled with adjectives. *The Stranger,* with nouns, perhaps. But this isn't very interesting, is it?

RCS: Is there anything in your writing that all your critics seem to have missed? Is that a sufficiently "interesting" question?

CAMUS: [*laughs appreciatively*] Yes, it is to me. They all seem to miss the humor. I am, after all, an ironic writer as well as being ghastly serious, which is all my readers seem to recognize—at least consciously.

RCS: You must admit that plague, murder, being condemned to death, drinking one's life away in Amsterdam—these aren't exactly the subjects of which great jokes are made.

CAMUS: On the contrary, they are the ultimate "jokes," if that's what you want to call them. It is in the extremes of life that a man finds happiness. Perhaps it is there that he finds humor too.

RCS: Certainly not on television, however!

CAMUS: Ah, your new American obsession. Soon it will devour you.

RCS: A happy death, anyway—our own form of innocence.

CAMUS: A fraudulent form of self-consciousness, I would say. Be that as it may, there's one question that I'm surprised you haven't asked.

RCS: What's that?

CAMUS: The question everyone always asks me. [*lowers his voice, attempting an American accent*] "M. Camus: Are you an existentialist?"

RCS: Yes, well, M. Camus, *are* you an existentialist?

CAMUS: [*with a hearty laugh—his first*] No, Monsieur, I am not an existentialist.

RCS: Why not?

CAMUS: Ah—you are serious again. But it is not a serious question. Why do I or do I not accept a name-tag that Sartre once proposed for himself? Would it not be curious—and most un-existential—if I were to do so?

RCS: I see the point. But you agree with Sartre that there is no God?

CAMUS: Yes, I do, but so did the Nazis. And there are some ex-istentialists—who sport that name as if they were joining a once-exclusive country club—who do believe in God, as you must know.

RCS: You mean Jaspers, for instance.

CAMUS: Yes, and Maritian; perhaps Buber; and in retrospect, although he, too—of all people—would reject the label, Kierkegaard.

RCS: And you do agree with Sartre that life is, to use your word, "absurd"?

CAMUS: Yes; he says, with a note of despair that I avoid, that "man is a useless passion."

RCS: You are both fervent individualists.

CAMUS: Yes. As Marx said, the individual will always be the point of departure. And happiness, I would add, the goal.

RCS: And, we have already established that you share Sartre's sense of responsibility, though he is abstract, you think . . .

CAMUS: A *dogmatist,* I would say . . .

RCS: And you are a humanist.

CAMUS: Sartre would claim that title, too; but what he means, I'm afraid, is simply that there is no God, no given purpose to human life. He does not insist, as I do, that a humanist is one who cares about individual human life, about each man's hap-piness, one who will not conspire in furthering the misery of man for any noble but abstract end.

RCS: I must ask, for you speak continually of "man" —man's fate, man's happiness, man's responsibility—what about *women*? What, if I may ask, about *Missus* Sisyphus?

CAMUS: [*a quick smile, then very serious*] Well, in French as in English, the word "man" is a general term including both men and women.

RCS: Yes, but you seem to evade the point. All your characters, for example, are men. Your women are silent.

CAMUS: As my mother was silent, but no less significant for that . . .

RCS: But the mother in *The Stranger* is dead when the novel begins. Meursault's girlfriend Marie is little but a pretty face, a warm body; we know her only by her smell, her giggle, her laugh.

CAMUS: Meursault isn't much more.

RCS: Yes, but Meursault is at least a character; Marie isn't even a foil.

CAMUS: That's true, but the mother's presence is what defines the novel.

RCS: It's true, that's so, but the point is, again, she isn't a *character*. And *The Plague:* it's all men. *The Fall,* a man; *The Myth of Sisyphus,* all about the absurd *man,* the absurd hero, Don Juan, Kafka, all men, often womanizing men.

CAMUS: I'm guilty, I suppose. There is Martha in my play *Malentendu,* but yes, you're right, and I admit, I distrust women. I am thoroughly dependent on them, but they do not share my world.

RCS: Would you say that existentialism is primarily a male philosophy?

CAMUS: That isn't my concern. But you might ask Simone.

RCS: Let me ask about your present plans. Are you writing at present?

CAMUS: I recently finished a translation of Faulkner's *Requiem for a Nun.*

RCS: Yes, and the general view is that you've undergone a Christian conversion—returned to the flock, so to speak.

CAMUS: If I had instead translated a Greek play, would the view be that I had come to believe in Zeus?

RCS: Touché! What *is* your attitude to Christianity at the moment?

CAMUS: A sense of alliance, actually. The church, too, is concerned with human suffering, and the Pope, at least, has the power to do something about it, which makes for a rather grand difference between us.

RCS: Beside the fact that you don't believe in God, of course.

CAMUS: Of course. The difference is that I am pessimistic about man's destiny, but optimistic about man. They are optimists about destiny, but pessimists about man. What the world awaits from Christianity is for it to speak loud and clear, to forget the abstract and face up to the bloodstained face of the present.

RCS: You quoted from a Japanese proverb a moment ago—

CAMUS: Hagakure.

RCS: Can an existentialist—if you'll pardon the expression—quote Hagakure in good conscience?

CAMUS: I've developed an intense interest in Zen, as a matter of fact, which I find a quite logical extension of my earlier ideas. I'm thinking of going to India someday soon.

RCS: I would like very much to see how that ties in with your book.

CAMUS: But I do not read my books. I want to move on to something else.

RCS: Another *café au lait,* perhaps?

CAMUS: No, I think I'll retreat to the *sauna,* in fact. I'm still a bit like a lizard, you know. If I can't have the sun—at least the Swedes provide the heat.

RCS: M. Camus, I've enjoyed talking with you. But one last question, if you will.

CAMUS: Surely.

RCS: Are you happy?

CAMUS: Yes, I am, and despite this drizzle. But it's a happiness that you Americans might not understand.

RCS: Well, we think happiness has to have a smile, you know. [*draws on the napkin the trademark of an American hamburger chain*— ☺]

Camus smiles broadly, ludicrously, then laughs and leaves the café. And I do feel, after all, that I've just met Clamence.

BIBLIOGRAPHY

Sartre

BASIC WORKS (IN ENGLISH TRANSLATIONS):

Transcendence of the Ego. Translated by F. Williams and R. Kirkpatrick. New York: 1957.

Imagination. Translated by F. Williams. Ann Arbor: 1962.

The Emotions: Outline of a Theory. Translated by B. Frechtman. New York: 1948.

Being and Nothingness. Translated by H. Barnes. New York: 1956.

Existentialism as a Humanism. Translated by P. Mairet. London: 1948.

Literary and Philosophical Essays. Translated by A. Michaelson. New York: 1962.

Portrait of the Anti–Semite. Translated by J. Becker. New York: 1948.

St. Genet: Actor and Martyr. Translated by B. Frechtman. New York: 1963.

Search for a Method. Translated by H. Barnes. New York: 1963.

Critique of Dialectical Reason. Translated by A. Sheridan-Smith. London: 1976.

NOVELS AND PLAYS OF PARTICULAR PHILOSOPHICAL INTEREST:

Nausea. Translated by L. Alexander. New York: 1949.

"The Wall." In *Intimacy.* Translated by L. Alexander. New York: 1952.

"No Exit," together with "The Flies," "Dirty Hands" and "The Respectful Prostitute." Translated by G. Steward and L. Abel. New York: 1947.

The Age of Reason and *The Reprieve.* Translated by E. Sutton. New York: 1947.

Troubled Sleep. Translated by G. Hopkins. New York: 1950.

The Devil and the Good Lord. Translated by K. Black. New York: 1960.

AUTOBIOGRAPHY:

The Words. Translated by B. Frechtman. New York: 1964.

"Sartre: An Interview." *New York Review of Books,* March 26, 1970, vol. XIV.

A FEW SECONDARY STUDIES:

Danto, Arthur. *Jean-Paul Sartre.* New York: 1975.

Desan, W. *The Tragic Finale.* New York: 1960.

Fell, Joseph. *Sartre's Theory of the Passions.* New York: 1962.

Grene, Marjorie. *Sartre.* New York: 1973.

Manser, Anthony. *Sartre: A Philosophical Study.* London: 1966.

Murdoch, Iris. *Sartre: Romantic Rationalist.* New Haven: 1953.

Warnock, M. *The Philosophy of Sartre.* London: 1955.

Heidegger

BASIC WORKS (IN ENGLISH TRANSLATIONS):

Being and Time. Translated by MacQuarrie and Robinson. New York: 1962.

Introduction to Metaphysics. Translated by R. Manheim. New Haven: 1958.

Kant and the Problem of Metaphysics. Translated by J. Churchill. Bloomington, Indiana: 1962.

A CONVENIENT COLLECTION:

Krell, D., ed. *Martin Heidegger: Basic Writings.* New York: 1977. Includes "What is Metaphysics?", "On the Essence of Truth," and "Letter on Humanism" (Heidegger's reply to Sartre) as well as other seminal essays.

A FEW SECONDARY STUDIES:

Barrett, W. *Irrational Man.* New York: 1958.

Grene, Marjorie. *Martin Heidegger.* London: 1957.

Kind, M. *Heidegger's Philosophy.* New York: 1964.

Langan, T. *The Meaning of Heidegger*. New York: 1959.

Macomber, H. *The Anatomy of Disillusion*. Evanston: 1967.

Marx, Werner. *Heidegger and the Tradition*. Evanston: 1971.

Olafson, F. *Principles and Persons*. Baltimore: 1967.

Schmitt, R. *Martin Heidegger on Being Human*. New York: 1969.

Versenyi, L. *Heidegger, Being and Truth*. New Haven: 1965.

ALSO:

Murray, Michael, ed. *Heidegger and Modern Philosophy*. New Haven: 1978.

Camus:

NOVELS AND PHILOSOPHICAL ESSAYS:

The Myth of Sisyphus. Translated by J. O'Brien. New York: 1955.

The Stranger. Translated by S. Gilbert. New York: 1946.

The Plague. Translated by S. Gilbert. New York: 1948.

The Rebel. Translated by A. Bower. New York: 1954.

The Fall. Translated by J. O'Brien. New York: 1957.

Resistance, Rebellion and Death. Translated by J. O'Brien. New York: 1961.

Caligula (And Other Plays). Translated by S. Gilbert. New York: 1958.

A FEW SECONDARY STUDIES:

Bree, G. *Camus*. New Brunswick: 1961.

Cruickshank, J. *Camus and the Literature of Revolt*. London: 1959.

Lottman, H. *Camus*. New York: 1979.

O'Brien, C. C. *Albert Camus*. New York: 1970.

Thody, P. *Camus: A Study of His Work*. London: 1957.